D1518435

NO
LAUGHING
MATTER

Other Books by Margaret Halsey
With Malice Toward Some
Some of My Best Friends Are Soldiers
Color Blind
The Folks at Home
This Demi-Paradise
The Pseudo-Ethic

NO
LAUGHING
MATTER

The Autobiography of a WASP

MARGARET HALSEY

J. B. Lippincott Company · Philadelphia and New York

Copyright © 1977 by Margaret Halsey
All rights reserved
First edition
9 8 7 6 5 4 3 2
Printed in the United States of America

U.S. Library of Congress Cataloging in Publication Data

Halsey, Margaret, birth date
   No laughing matter.

   SUMMARY: An autobiographical account of what it meant
to be a WASP in America during four decades encompassing
the Depression, World War II, McCarthyism, and Watergate.
   1. Halsey, Margaret, 1910- 2. United States—
Biography. [1. Halsey, Margaret, birth date
2. United States—Biography] I. Title.
CT275.H28743A36 974.7'04'0924 [B] [92] 77-22949
ISBN-0-397-01240-3

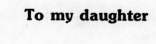
To my daughter

Contents

Author's Note

An effort has been made in the following pages to be as truthful as human fallibility permits, but for the sake of various people's privacy, some of the names of still-living individuals have been altered.

Introduction

We have heard a great deal from Jewish writers about what it means to come from a Jewish background, but so far not much has been written about growing up WASP. For the ethnic minorities in the United States, the problem is to climb up; but for the WASPs—who were once, but are no longer, the dominant group in the culture—the problem is to climb down. No one has yet commented on it, but Richard Nixon—with a little help from John Erlichmann—killed once and for all the idea that a white Anglo-Saxon Protestant is physically better looking and morally more reliable than a person who is not a white Anglo-Saxon Protestant.

The WASPs, then, are an endangered species; but they differ from tigers and elephants in that they endangered themselves. However, no privileged caste just simply disappears overnight. The WASP-dominated United States came to grief with its unconsciously arrogant adventure in Vietnam, but by common consent nobody remembers Vietnam any more. The emergence of the Third World seems to have made the climbing down of the WASPs inevitable, both at home and abroad. But just how they climb down is a matter of considerable interest, for giving up alcohol or cigarettes is

11

a lead-pipe cinch compared to the renunciation of complacence by a former (self-appointed) elite.

The cutting down to size of the WASPs being a matter
of historical necessity, it seemed as if an examination of
WASP conditioning and WASP consciousness (so far as the
latter goes) might be of interest and significance. But is that
enough of a credential for an autobiography? Many personal
histories, for instance, are enlivened by a fund of anecdotes
about the Great, and these I cannot supply. The Great and I
sometimes met, but we never seemed to get to the point of
exchanging telephone numbers. On the other hand, I have,
in a success-oriented society, known what it is to have a notable success. In 1938, the year before World War II broke
out, I published a humorous book about the English called
With Malice Toward Some which caught my compatriots on
their collective funnybone and was a runaway best seller.
Long before today's pop stars, I experienced the delight and
some of the difficulties of the sudden vault into the spotlight.

I did not follow up this first success with more humor,
because, through a special set of circumstances, I got very
much interested in race relations, and having in full measure
the WASP's guilt about non-WASPs, I brought out in 1946 a
book called *Color Blind* which was a plea for racial equality.
In 1946, black militants, black power, Rosa Parks and Watts
were still far in the future; and though the civil rights movement of the 1960s made *Color Blind* entirely out of date, it
was in its prehistoric time something of a ground-breaker.

Once having embarked on a serious kind of writing, I
seemed impelled to keep on with it and in the 1950s devoted
myself to a stubborn defense of various liberal causes.

But why go off on this tack, when there had been so
much money in the humor?

Partly because I am one of those people who take their
politics seriously, but mainly because new and unprec-

edented conditions developed in the decade after the
war—McCarthyism, permissiveness, consumerism and the
threat of nuclear annihilation. Intuition told me that, in this
altered climate, my kind of old-fashioned, Mark Twainish
humor was soon going to be stone cold dead in the market.
And indeed it was. The Will Rogers–Robert Benchley tradi-
tion in which my generation was reared became one with
Nineveh and Tyre, and the "sick" or "black" humor which
succeeded it I was too apple-cheeked and innocent to produce.

    In 1963, I published a slim volume called *The
Pseudo-Ethic*. It was subtitled "A Speculation about American Politics and Morals" and its argument was that if politics
and morals came to a definitive parting of the ways, as
seemed to be the case, the political system would lose all
credence. Political morality, as a matter of fact, was a subject
that greatly exercised me—and with particular reference to
my fellow-WASP, Mr. Nixon. In 1958, after Eisenhower
had his heart attack, there had been a great deal of talk about
"the new Nixon," and at that time *The New Republic* printed
an article of mine which affirmed passionately that there was
not a new Nixon and there was never going to be. A Nixon
Administration, the article predicted, would be staffed by
other Nixons and it would be *Walpurgisnacht* on the
Potomac. Sixteen years later, when Watergate came along,
the article was resurrected and was cited in various public
prints as an example of great political foresight.

    But that is by the way, for on the personal as distinct
from the political side, I have had less reason to be self-
congratulatory. For many years I was a wife and mother in
an American suburb, at the same time writing in a terribly
earnest way on thought-provoking subjects. Naturally, these
well-meant efforts did not reach the same wide and almost
hysterically eager public as had been reached by the humor-

ous *With Malice*, and the praise, plaudits and excitement attendant upon the publication of that first book seemed in later years to have sunk gradually into oblivion, leaving no trace. But the popular success of *With Malice* did actually leave a long-lasting trace, for it made a domestic tyrant of me.

To be sure, the tyrannizing potential had to exist in my character in the first place, but under different circumstances it might have remained dormant. Bestsellerdom, however, brought it to an advanced state of development; and while in the outside world I could not say "Boo!" to a goose, at home with my husband and daughter I was a one-woman multinational. It took me a long time to realize this, and in the meantime I pursued many a false hypothesis as to why I was not experiencing the happiness to which my good intentions entitled me. When I finally understood the extent to which I was a personal imperialist, I had perforce to climb down, so that in an odd way my tiny personal history has seemed to parallel the recent history of my country.

Any kind of upbringing—Jewish or Gentile, rich or poor, Occidental or Oriental—leaves claw marks on the up-bringee, and the Martin Luther–Cotton Mather syndrome has much to answer for in terms of authoritarianism, obsession and hypocrisy. On the other hand, the liberated people of today, though noticeably different from their predecessors, do not seem noticeably superior as a human type. Purposefully hedonist, immune to guilt feelings, doing their own thing, living entirely in the now and scornfully dismissive of anything that happened before breakfast time this morning, they seem, like the astronauts in outer space, to suffer from weightlessness.

But perhaps—unsuspected by us all—there is in operation a moral equivalent to the law of gravity. Perhaps we can only feel natural and completely ourselves if we are made heavy by inhibitions, by a feeling of responsibility for others, by a sense of our debt to the past, by the ideal of untarnished honor and by the ability to suffer from the pangs of conscience. Whatever happens to the WASPs, they have deserved it; but it might be a mere matter of common sense to sift out of their streaky legacy whatever it contains of proven usefulness.

NO
LAUGHING
MATTER

1
How to Raise a Prig

My mother was a woman who used to say, in a studiously quiet voice, "I pride myself on my reserve." My father, on the other hand, had no more reserve than a Force 9 gale. Their marriage was an unqualified disaster, but the neighbors were not supposed to know it. When my father started denouncing his womenfolk—my mother, my sister and me—for everything from laziness and ingratitude to deliberately hiding his Stillson wrench, my mother ran around and closed all the windows.

My mother wanted everybody to think that our household was one of unimpeachable dignity, where all human passion was completely under control. That kind of façade was difficult to maintain, however, when you lived, as we did, in a two-family house. My father had built the house in 1910, the year I was born. He was German on his mother's side—his first name was Reinhold—and although he was a violent man, both physically and verbally, he was also cautious and provident. The income from the extra apartment would cover the payments on the mortgage.

The two-family house was in a remote and straggling suburb of Yonkers, New York. It was an Edward Hopper landscape. There was a great deal of space and—those being the days before air pollution—a great deal of bright, clear light shining down on commonplace, humdrum objects: frame and stucco houses, unpaved roads, an isolated little grocery store.

As we think of suburbs today, the word seems too strong for such an unimposing little community. It meandered over two shallow hills. At the bottom between the hills was a marsh (now drained) and a spur railroad (now disused) that ran to New York. The city of Yonkers proper was a mile or two away. It was reached by a trolley line which looped down and up the hills in splendid arcs that made the wheels scream, and the motorman always clanged his bell vociferously as he courted derailment on the curves.

In the opposite direction from Yonkers was land so vacant, featureless and useless-looking that one could not imagine anyone's ever having gone to the trouble of taking title to it. Someone evidently had, however, because today it has disappeared under rows of tightly packed houses. But in my childhood the unpromising acreage was almost blank, save for a dreary reservoir—mounded and fenced in, so you could not see the water—and a small, unprosperous farm.

After I learned to read, I became conscious of the deficiencies of this landscape. Our family had pretensions to culture. We had a sepia portrait of the Coliseum hanging over the umbrella stand in the front hall and, in the living room, two glass-fronted bookcases containing among other things the works of James Fenimore Cooper and Sir Walter Scott. My father had had to leave school and go to work when he was twelve, but my mother had gone to normal school and taught third grade before she was married. This little library was partly books my father had bought to educate himself and partly the residue of my mother's young womanhood. I read and reread Cooper and Scott, and they made me dissatisfied with the immediate environment. I longed for virgin forests, rushing torrents and scowling crags.

Vacant lots separated the scattered houses. Since the automobile had not yet come into general use, there was no litter of beer bottles or old newspapers; but builders had left occasional rusty boilers, abandoned sinks and piles of discarded pipe. June brought a redeeming crop of daisies and black-eyed Susans and in September there were goldenrod and purple asters, but the vegetation ran a good deal to burdock and thistles, with an occasional clump of sumac. Nevertheless, I always referred to the empty lots as "meadows."

Our little community was called Lincoln Park, and while my sister and I were growing up, Lincoln Park was growing, too—but slowly. When a new house was to be built, a crew of Italian laborers came to dig out the cellar. They talked their native tongue, and for lunch they ate the kind of sandwiches which are now called submarines. On both scores, we children learned to look down on them. They were not an "ethnic group." They were just foreigners.

If there was a house under construction, the children played in it after the workmen had gone home—getting splinters from the rough ladders, teetering on the beams before the floors were laid, and breathing in the pungent smell of raw lumber. We did not vandalize these houses. They were "property," and we children had learned from our elders to pronounce the very word with a special, reverent inflection. However, we carried away discarded bits of lumber and used them in combination with tattered awnings and other things we found in the vacant lots to build huts.

The Lincoln Park landscape was bleak, but it was excellent terrain for the game of cops and robbers because of the tall weeds. And although it was largely treeless, except for a stretch of thinnish woodland near the reservoir, an occasional lonely apple tree or isolated oak invited climbing.

The streets were lit by gas, and every evening a man came
around with a lighter on a long pole and ignited the lamp-
wicks. The lamp poles were too smooth for successful shin-
nying, but a lamppost was usually "home" when we played
tag.

We did not play baseball. It was too hard to round up
enough players all at once. Many of the Lincoln Park families had children, but there were not many families; the
houses were far apart; and not everybody had a telephone.
However, in winter the swamp froze over and there would be
clear patches the size of our dining room rugs on which we
could skate. In summer we played mumblety-peg on people's
lawns. After I learned to swim—at a Girl Scout camp that
cost seven dollars a week—I was passionate about the water
and fretted during the long summer vacations because there
was no place nearby to swim.

In the spring we caught tadpoles in a sullen little brook
in the woods that usually disappeared when the hot weather
came. Sometimes after school the girls went to the woods
and gathered spring flowers—violets, hepaticas, bloodroot
and Dutchman's breeches. On one of these flower-gathering
excursions another little girl told me that babies came from
some kind of friction between a man and a woman, a bit of
(unsolicited) information to which I gave no credence. There
was a lot of friction between my mother and father—they
said so themselves—and it did not produce any babies.

Sometimes one of the neighborhood families bought a
small tent from the Army and Navy store and put it up in the
back yard for the children to play in. One day a boy suggested that he and I should go into his tent and undress, so
that we could see each other's genitals. I was not much
drawn to the idea—he was a boy nobody liked—but I agreed.
Once inside, I said that he should go first. When he was
naked, however, I had scarcely a glance for the little convex

dimple of his penis because his chest was a mass of scar tis-
sue. He had been burned as a baby, he said. The thickened,
tortured skin appalled and fascinated me. It looked like sculp-
tured scrambled eggs.

When it was my turn to undress, I backed down. The
boy made no particular fuss. He merely shrugged. As I
crawled out of the tent and the flap fell behind me, I was
suddenly suffused with conscious virtue, a sensation to which
I have never been a stranger. I glowed with self-approval at
not having kept my part of the bargain. To the best of my
recollection, this was my debut as a prig.

One very happy part of my childhood was the comfortable awareness that there were people in the world who were
not as good as I. I was indebted for a certain part of this
awareness to a family named Terwilliger, who lived on the
down-at-heels farm near the reservoir. The Terwilligers had
no running water or electricity and they had too many children. Their dooryard was muddy, their fences dilapidated
and their small house and its outbuildings were falling down.
To me, they were Poverty Incarnate. It was to be many years
before anybody had the idea of the welfare state and social security, and the concept I formed of poverty, from hearing the
grown-ups refer to it, was that it was contagious and one had
better stay as far away from it as possible.

If there were people in the world who were not as good
as I, there were also people in the world who were better—a
fact which I accepted without resentment and without feeling
any particular challenge. Beyond Lincoln Park, in South
Yonkers, was a suburb called Park Hill. Park Hill was rocky
and romantically steep. Its tree-shaded streets curved pictur-
esquely past big Victorian houses set in extensive grounds. It
was one of the areas where the old families of Yonkers lived,
and some of the people there had automobiles. (They were
still called automobiles, and not cars.) There were virtually

no contacts between Lincoln Park and Park Hill unless somebody from Park Hill ran for public office and gave us the
chance to vote for him.

The children of Lincoln Park did not have the advantages of either country life or city life, but there was one way
in which we were lucky, and that was in our school. Surpris-
ingly, since the community was so sparsely settled, there was
a public school half a block from our house. The rumor was
that an alderman who owned the land had sold it to the city
at a handsome profit, but who got the idea of building a
school in the municipal Siberia that was Lincoln Park, nobody ever said.

Classes at P.S. 21 were so small that my parents liked to
say it was just as if we children were going to private school,
we got so much individual attention. The teachers were all
women, of course. Some were young and pretty; some
middle-aged and seasoned disciplinarians; but what gave the
school its special quality was the principal, Miss Sibley.

Everyone in the neighborhood looked up to Miss Sibley.
She had warmth and wisdom. No matter to whom she was
talking, grown-up or child, she seemed always aware of that
person's humanness and individuality. In my class there was
a wild, handsome, sullen Irish boy named Barry McCabe
who, to the incredulous horror of us conformists, was im-
pudent to the teachers and once even threatened to hit one of
them. Only Miss Sibley could tame Barry McCabe and get
him to do his homework. The word the parents always applied to her was "remarkable."

Lincoln Park was a lonely neighborhood and the grown-
ups, it appeared, wanted to keep it that way. When I was still
in the early years of grammar school, the New York subway
was extended to Van Cortlandt Park, which was only a little
over a mile from where we lived. There was a great outcry in
the community. "The Jews will come!" It seemed to be taken

for granted that everybody who lived in New York was Jewish.

After the subway came to Van Cortlandt, we had hikers on Sunday. Halfway down the hill from our house was an aqueduct. At least, it was always called "the aqueduct," though the pipes were underground and all that was visible was a broad flat strip of green. The aqueduct started at Van Cortlandt Park and ran northward for several miles, and it was an excellent place for walking. On a Sunday morning we would see people striding purposefully along it, sometimes with knapsacks on their backs. If they wore glasses, we looked at each other and said, "Jews."

Later in life I was to find out through personal involvement a little bit of what that cast-iron bigotry meant to the people against whom it was directed. At the time, however, I was conscious only that there was a pecking order even in the sacred congregation of the Gentiles. Our family were Episcopalians, and our parents assured my sister and me that Episcopalianism was superior to all other forms of worship. My father with tolerant humor referred to Baptists, Methodists and Presbyterians as "the dissenting sects." My mother said that the Episcopal service was more beautiful, dignified and time-honored than anybody else's and that its adherents were more "cultured"—a word my family used regularly and with perfect seriousness. My response to this indoctrination was that of the Pharisees I heard about in Sunday school. I thanked God I was not as other men.

In Lincoln Park in the years before and during World War I the two most familiar institutions were God and constipation. Every day mothers asked their children in a low, embarrassed voice if the children had moved their bowels. But if constipation was an enemy, the Deity was a trusted ally, and "What religion are you?" was one of the first questions asked of a new child in the neighborhood.

One year a French family moved in. They had a daughter named Yvonne. I put the usual inquiry to Yvonne,
though without much interest in the answer. I was merely
waiting impatiently till I could spring my Episcopalianism on
her.

Yvonne surprised me. "We're Free-Thinkers," she
said—only with her French accent, it came out "Fwee-
Tinkers."

"What's that?"

"We don't believe in God."

I must have broken the world's record for the standing
backward jump. But when nothing happened—when
Yvonne did not shrivel up with leprosy or drop dead at my
feet—I finally said tentatively, "Let's play."

What goes into the making of a prig? The Lincoln Park
community—isolated, narrow and provincial—was a favor-
able climate for the development of prigs; but my sister, a
year younger than I, lived there too and did not grow up to
be didactic, whereas I did. She and I responded in different
ways to a polarized household. My father was driving, perfec-
tionist, Teutonically methodical and with about the same tolerance for frustration as a hungry tiger. My mother, on the
other hand, was passive and inert. She had, however, what
Dylan Thomas's widow once described as "the terrible
strength of the weak."

My mother was almost a recluse. Other children were
not permitted to come into our house because they might
track dirt in. I think the real reason was that my mother was
afraid they would report on us to their parents. She would
not invite people to visit us because, she said, she was
ashamed of how shabby our furnishings were. Actually, they
were no shabbier than anybody else's. Nor would she go out

and visit other people. "I'm not a mixer," she said. She went to church regularly, but took no part in any church activity, and she never set foot in our tenants' apartment or invited them into ours. If you get intimate with people, she said, quarrels are likely to develop. It was better to keep them at a distance.

My mother made great sacrifices for her children, and, unlike my father, she was not forever pointing them out. For years, when my sister and I were little, she went without new clothes and did not get her teeth fixed so that money could be saved to send us to college. But my memory of her is bracketed by two remarks that came nearly forty years apart.

I started school at the age of four, and the first day I went to kindergarten, my mother sent me alone. I walked up to the building with dry mouth and pounding heart. It seemed to me the hugest thing I had ever seen. I did not know which of its gaping doors to go in or what to do when I got inside. To make matters worse, I stumbled and fell going up the steps. Some boys were racketing around the school yard and one of them yelled at me, "Come here and I'll pick you up." The other boys were enchanted with this witticism and converted it into a jeering chorus.

Bursting into tears, I ran back home and asked my mother to convoy me to the school.

"Certainly not, I'm doing the laundry," she said.

Many years later, when my father was seventy-six and in the hospital with what proved to be his final illness, she was telephoned and told she ought to get to his bedside because he was growing weaker.

"I can't," she said. "I'm doing the laundry."

When my mother was a young matron, not much was understood about the role of fantasy in people's lives. But looking back I can see that her almost morbid withdrawal from human contacts was due to the fact that she lived with a pervasive, abiding and unshakable fantasy. Human contacts disturbed it. Hence she avoided them.

My mother cooked and scrubbed and varnished floors and washed and ironed and sewed, like the other women in the neighborhood. But in her mind she was "a perfect lady" and an aristocrat. That was why she never raised her voice, never cried and never showed emotion. In her lexicon the sin against the Holy Ghost was to do anything that made you conspicuous. People did not talk about role-playing in those days, but never was a role played to the hilt like my mother's secret role as the Lady Prioress of Lincoln Park.

Her parents had christened her Annie and she hated it because it was a servant's name. But her parents had been more prescient than they knew. In real life Annie had the perfect servant mentality. She was industrious, unimaginative and limited intellectually, and she liked to be told what to do. When pressure was put on her to go to her dying husband in the hospital, she complied immediately.

"Of course, if you think I should," she said, "I'd better do it."

The foregoing, of course, are the perceptions of later life. As a child, I worshiped my mother. In our unvisited household there was no one else around to compete with her for possession of my feelings. In every way I could, I fed and supported Annie's predominating fantasy. So clearly did the Lady Prioress come through to me—at the ironing board, over the washtubs—that I tied myself into knots trying to live up to her simplistic idea of "a lady." When she let fall remarks about how badly my father treated her, I burned with anger on her behalf. Partisanship was something I learned very young and have been swayed by ever since.

My mother turned aside all inquiries about her early life, so I can only speculate on what made her what she was.

She had an older brother and a younger sister, both of whom were "mixers," and her father, who had been a foreman in a silk mill, used to stop in a saloon for a glass of beer and a little fraternizing on the way home from work. My maternal grandfather was the most temperate of men, but this glass of beer was once mentioned to me by Annie as a cross her mother had to bear.

My mother's mother died before my sister and I were old enough to say "grandmother." We called her Gumma. "Gumma was like me," my mother said, apropos of my grandfather's glass of beer. "She was not a mixer." I can only explain Annie by assuming that she was a replica of her own mother and that she imitated and idealized her own mother much as I imitated and idealized her.

The odd thing about Gumma was that, except for Annie, none of her next of kin ever mentioned her. My grandfather survived her by thirty years, but I never heard him speak of her. There were no anecdotes about her, no favorite recipes handed down, no shawl that everybody remembered seeing her in. She seems to have been a cipher, without either accomplishments or vices, who passed through life without leaving a trace.

Unless my mother's character was a trace.

Gumma, I learned from Annie, had been brought up in Scotland in some sort of strict Calvinist sect whose members attended church three times each Sunday and cooked all the food for Sunday on Saturday, so as not to break the Sabbath. I seem to catch an echo of that life-denying Calvinism in a favorite remark of my mother's. When Annie hung up the dish towels, after finishing the dinner dishes at night, she often said with a little expulsion of breath, "Well! One day's journey nearer the grave."

Alfred North Whitehead once spoke of "the curse of the need to worship," and because of the need to worship I had

to keep myself from the knowledge of my mother's real character. Sometimes, however, that knowledge came close to
breaking through. In one of my early years in grammar
school, the other apartment in our house was rented to a
young couple named Mr. and Mrs. Paul. By sheer force of
fantasy Annie had transformed Reinhold's household into a
sort of secular nunnery, but there were ways in which even
Annie could not bend the environment to her will. Mrs.
Paul got pregnant.

I can imagine the dismay—the terror, really—with
which my mother must have heard this news. The children
would ask questions! In those days pregnancy was not the
unremarkable phenomenon it is now. Pregnant women—at
least in Lincoln Park—tacitly agreed that their "condition"
was in some way shameful and often asked other women to
shop for them, so as to appear in public as little as possible.

Annie need not have worried. The children did not ask
questions. How she got it across to us, I do not know, but to
me—and I believe to my sister—the directive was unmistakable. No notice was to be taken, even in our thoughts. Then
one day I came running in for supper and found Annie looking flustered and not at all like a Lady Prioress.

"Women-get-very-sick-when-they-have-babies," she said,
all in one breath. "Will you go down to the railroad station
and tell Mr. Paul that his wife has gone to the hospital?"

She handed me a fifty-cent piece.

To my own astonishment, I said, "No," and handed it
back.

In our frugal household fifty cents was the wealth of the
Indies, but I was outraged by the inconsistency. I had played
the rules of the game. Even in my thoughts I had made Mrs.
Paul's pregnancy nonexistent. Now I was being asked to go
out and proclaim it in public. The very size of the reward
made it clear that I was being offered a bribe. My mother was

not doing the laundry. She had nothing cooking on the stove. She was asking me to go because she was too embarrassed to go herself.

She did not press me. She asked my sister, who accepted with alacrity.

For one brief moment, I had seen Annie as she really was. The insight was intolerable and had the effect of redoubling my idealization. As a child, there was only one tiny way in which I had a realistic perception of my mother. I knew by intuition that when she was a young woman teaching school, she had never expected anyone to ask her to marry. But not until many years later did I understand that her obtuseness, her fantasizing and her dwarfish barbarisms sprang, basically, from despair.

If much was lacking at home, a great deal of the deficiency was made up for at school. To me school was a daily release from prison. There, if you made an effort, you could count on its being applauded and not merely taken for granted as no more than you ought to do. On the playground of P.S. 21 I learned, from the teachers, that it was necessary to be a good sport about losing. Or at least to *appear* to be a good sport. I could never in my heart shrug off defeat as "just a game," and my idea of fair play was when my side won. However, I learned to dissemble—though what unsportsmanlike feelings churned underneath!—and was rewarded by not being the last one chosen when captains selected their teams.

In the sixth grade I had a teacher who showed me how to write. Her name was Mrs. Kelly, and she was enormously fat and assertively Irish. Being Irish would have counted heavily against her in Lincoln Park save that, by some sleight of hand we children did not understand, she was Protestant and not Catholic. Mrs. Kelly could be egregiously sentimental, but she also had a fearsome temper. When she berated a class, she could be heard two blocks away.

Mrs. Kelly's temper made me cringe, but it did not keep me from learning what she had to teach. She showed me what was wrong with a sentence like "I have a luscious pear tree" (inspired by my pleased discovery of the word "luscious" with its captivating spelling). She taught me the beginnings of paragraph structure. From her I learned that a pronoun must relate unmistakably to its antecedent. She applauded the use of synonyms, so that the same noun did not recur three times in eight lines, but discouraged putting four adjectives in a row because they were all too lovely to be left out.

It was Miss Sibley, however, who was the most pervasive influence, not only on me, but on everyone. She was tall and round-shouldered, with squashy features, but she had beautiful teeth—in those days a less common asset than it is now—and deep-set brown eyes. I idolized her. I used sometimes to walk over to South Yonkers just so that I could pass lingeringly in front of the apartment building where she lived.

The other pupils in P.S. 21 were not so rapture-prone as I, but when Miss Sibley spoke in the weekly Assembly, she swayed them. She often talked in Assembly about Abraham Lincoln, whom she venerated. At that time there was a standard repertoire of Lincoln stories that all children were told: about his retracing his steps a mile to release a squealing pig stuck under a fence; about his walking back ten miles to return some money he had mistakenly been paid in excess; about his having said, when told that General Grant drank too much, that he would like to find out what kind of whiskey the General favored, so that he could send a barrel of it to his other generals.

By today's standards Miss Sibley's picture of Lincoln was

idealized; but our self-indulgent age dismantles heroes, not wholly out of love of truth but also in order not to feel reproached by them. In P.S. 21 we learned to think of Lincoln as humorous, self-deprecating, tenderhearted, scrupulously honest and unswervingly principled. If he was not in reality as unswervingly principled as we believed, we were still better off than the children, several generations later, whose elders' idea of respect and admiration was encompassed in "I like Ike."

Like Lincoln himself, Miss Sibley was anti-prig. Not only for me but for the other children, she counteracted some of the narrowness and rigidity of our Lincoln Park homes. Miss Sibley, eschewing the universal disapproval, referred to the outlaw Barry McCabe with equanimity and even admiration. The second grade was taught by a young and attractive teacher named Miss Abeloff. Once some of us overheard Miss Sibley, talking to her staff, speak with great pity and tenderness of having had to break the news to Miss Abeloff that her father had died. This was instructive, because Miss Abeloff was Jewish and therefore presumably incapable of feeling the loss of a father.

Miss Sibley's warmth melted even my mother, who did the absolutely unprecedented thing, for her, of inviting the principal to dinner several times while I was in grammar school. My father had been president of the P.T.A. for several years, and I remember Miss Sibley standing in our small living room, relaxed and smiling, and saying, "Your father is a wonderful man."

I was dumbstruck. I had had intimations, which I disregarded, that not everyone shared Annie's view of Reinhold. My father had also been president of the Lincoln Park Civic Association and in that role had virtually single-handedly prevented the installation of a sewage-disposal plant

in our shallow valley. I had heard some of the neighbors say
admiringly that Mr. Halsey had brains, but the neighbors
were not Miss Sibley.

My first impulse was to defend my mother. "You don't
know what he's like at home!" was the sentence that leaped
to mind, but was left unuttered. If Miss Sibley admired my
father, and he was mine, it was a bond between us.

Miss Sibley must have had human failings, but I was
not in a position to see them. She had a younger sister
named Elfrieda who had been divorced. Once, dashing into
the cloakroom for a sweater during recess, I overheard Mrs.
Kelly saying angrily, "She's weak. She lets Elfrieda walk all
over her. She spoils her." I was ravaged with jealousy. Elfrieda had blotted her copybook. She was divorced. She did
not deserve to be spoiled by Miss Sibley. Why couldn't that
heavenly fate have been reserved for me?

Miss Sibley died of cancer when I was twenty-seven. I
was living in England at the time—having in the interval
managed by some miracle to evade my Yonkersonian destiny—and I spent a long afternoon in that foreign land remembering her. She was the principal of a very small school
in a godforsaken suburb of an unimportant town, but what
would Lincoln Park have been without her? I do not know
whether her generous sympathies saved Barry McCabe from
the life of crime that was confidently predicted for him, but
they certainly helped to save me from being a third-genera-
tion Gumma.

One of the things that was lacking at home was any kind
of relationship between my sister and me. This was partly
because I was smug and pious. One day when Mary and I
had been fighting—rolling over and over on the lawn, biting
and kicking each other—my mother came running out of the

house and said, "That's *disgusting!* What will the neighbors think?" I stood up and, striving as ever to get into Annie's good graces, quoted a line I had heard in Sunday school. "Let not the sun go down upon thy wrath," I said with conscious precocity. Annie beamed. My sister stalked away.

Mary must have found me insufferable, but nobody in those days knew anything about sibling rivalry. The Innocence of Children was considered a part of nature itself, and mothers used to say admonishingly to their quarreling offspring, "Birds in their little nests agree." I for my part found my sister baffling. She did not worship Annie, did not take her part against Reinhold, and did not give a damn about Annie's ideal of being a lady. She was indifferent to Reinhold's rages, and when Mrs. Kelly yelled at her for having skimped on her homework, and ordered her to come back from lunch half an hour early and do it properly, she reported the fact to my mother with a shrug and took her own time about returning. She hated eggs, and when my father commanded her to finish them—the clean plate, it goes without saying, was an inflexible rule—she waited calmly till he had left the table and then scraped them into the garbage pail. I would sooner have flung myself in front of a railroad train.

Only very rarely did we converge in a children's alliance against our parents, though a strong sense of unity was always evoked by a book on mythology called Bulfinch's *Age of Fable*. We read it together, lying on our stomachs on the floor. Bulfinch contained a few dim photographs of famous pieces of Greek statuary, and the beauty of these illustrations was that they were "classical" and could therefore be stared at without fear of reproach. We goggled at the bared breasts and wondered just what, exactly, was under the fig leaf. This reaction we were very much aware of having in common, though we communicated it only by sliding our eyes around to each other. But for the most part, we seemed to live in different worlds.

My sister grew up to be a handsome woman, and the pictures in our family photograph album show her to have been an exceptionally appealing baby, with a dark-eyed ingenuousness that smote the heart. Nor were we at all unequally endowed. When we were about seven and eight, we were taken down to Columbia University and given the old Stanford-Binet intelligence test, and we came out exactly even. Nevertheless, I was skipped twice while going through grammar school and Mary was not. Years later, when she was grown up, my sister told me in her uninflected way that she had been jealous of those promotions, but she gave no sign of it at the time.

All families have their legends—irreversible and sometimes disastrously wrong. The legend in our house was that Mary was Reinhold's favorite. He was indulgent with her as he was not with me. If I came home from school with a less than 99 average—which I often did, because I could not master arithmetic—he roared at me that if I did not try harder, he would turn me out into the street. Mary's marks were just average, but he accepted them without comment. If she overspent her allowance and asked him for more money, he occasionally gave it to her, though in the same circumstances all I got was a lecture on the value of a dollar.

One signal honor, however, my father did bestow on me and not on my sister. Flowers from a florist were unheard of in our community, except for funerals, but every year on my birthday Reinhold brought me home a dozen pink carnations. This favoritism Mary appeared not to notice, but she was inscrutable and nobody knew (or cared) what went on beneath her apparently low-keyed exterior.

On the surface, my sister seemed to have the more enviable position in the family. But the reality was that Mary—that adorable baby, that intelligent little girl—inherited Annie's basic despair. She early resigned herself to the family atmosphere of lovelessness and gave up any attempt to get real instead of mechanical attention from our parents. I on the other hand never stopped trying. My sister's childhood was a muted tragedy. Mine, despite its seeming rigors, was shot through with optimism.

My father was the antidote to the eventlessness which Annie imposed on our household. He had a good presence—he was tall and looked a little like Woodrow Wilson—and merely getting him off to work in the morning was like a mob scene in a Cecil B. DeMille movie. He stood in our dark, cramped front hall like a monarch dispatching equerries, and the equerries had to proceed at a fast gallop because the 7:56 could be heard whistling three miles up the line.

Somebody had to run for the shoe brush and give his shoes a last buff. Somebody else had to get a duster and wipe the fingerprints off his briefcase. If he discovered a hangnail, the nail scissors must be fetched. A bit of shaving cream in front of his ear? Get one of the face towels and *hurry!* His clean handkerchief had to be brought, and if it was badly ironed—as with poor Annie's luckless touch it might be—he said, "God damn it, do you expect me to go out of the house with *that?*"

He had to be brushed from top to toe until he was as free of lint as a surgeon's scalpel, and in winter we helped him into his overcoat. When he had to grope for the sleeve—we were all too short to be of real help—he rolled his eyes to the ceiling and asked the Deity what made us so stupid. But when, finally, he had put on his hat and adjusted it with

whole-souled concentration in front of the mirror, he suddenly relaxed and was apparently unaware that he had been
anything but good-natured.

Nobody saw the absurdity of it—this regal, Lear-like
performance played out in a minuscule hallway, with a back-
drop of hatrack, umbrella stand and sepia portrait of the
Coliseum. As the door closed after him, my mother said bitterly, "The Great I-Am," and I quoted a school-yard taunt:

> "I love me,
> I love me,
> I'm wild about myself . . ."

However, if I happened to glance out of the window and see
Reinhold crossing the vacant lots—eating up the ground with
a long, swinging stride—I had a fleeting awareness that he
lived up to standards and I was secretly proud of him.

My most vivid memory of him is tiny and seemingly inconsequential, but it also had to do with living up to standards. One night after we were all asleep there was a loud but
unidentifiable noise in the cellar. (At that time we lived in
the apartment on the first floor.) The noise woke me and my
parents, though not Mary. My father turned on the hall light
and as he passed my sister's and my darkened room, I could
see that he was afraid.

He had a grim but hangdog look, and young as I was, I
could feel as if it were in myself the conflict between his fear
and his sense of responsibility. When he got to the cellar,
there was nothing and nobody there. The noise was all the
more inexplicable because Reinhold locked the house up like
a fortress every night before he went to bed. But the incident
showed me very early in life something about my father I was
never to forget. He could make himself do what he was afraid
to do.

He was also an independent man, as he showed during

World War I. Even before the United States declared war on Germany, anti-German feeling ran so high that orchestras would not play Wagner and Beethoven and sauerkraut was renamed "liberty cabbage." Reinhold, however, took great pride in his German ancestry—his mother had been some kind of Prussian autocrat, fallen on evil days—and he would not go along with the popular frenzy.

He was not, in the phrase of the time, "pro-German." He took and passed with flying colors an examination which would have made him a major in the Corps of Engineers, and then was rejected by the Army because of poor eyesight. But when a deputation of citizens waited on him and suggested that if he wanted them to believe in his patriotism, he would do well to call himself Reginald instead of Reinhold, he declined. How he managed these zealots I do not know, but there were no repercussions that we children were aware of.

I was four years old when World War I broke out and would have had little consciousness of it save that a woman named Mrs. Loeffler moved into the house next door. Mrs. Loeffler was a Vassar graduate, and she was in real life the Lady Prioress type that Annie dreamed of being. Lincoln Park was obviously not her natural habitat, but she was married to a German who had been caught in Europe at the outbreak of the war and who was fighting in the German Army.

Reinhold was the only person in Lincoln Park who made her acquaintance. Everybody else patriotically ostracized her, but Reinhold said she was behaving admirably in a difficult situation. He went to her house every Saturday afternoon and they drank cocoa and read Heine and Schiller aloud in German. Mrs. Loeffler told me that Reinhold's accent was exceptionally pure.

"It's dogged as does it." We talk today about upward

mobility, but the phrase seems too shallow to describe the
years of slogging, grinding labor Reinhold put himself
through because he was determined not to spend all his life
as a factory hand—which was the way he started out. In
those days factory hands worked much longer hours than
they do now, but my father took correspondence school
courses and studied at night until eventually he was able to
leave the factory and go to work as a draftsman for a firm of
architects. It was a long and lonely pull, however, especially
since much of that time he was the sole support of his
mother, two sisters, and a brother.

After a few years with the architectural firm, he went to
work for the Bureau of Buildings of the Board of Education
of the City of New York, where he remained for thirty-one
years. Eventually he was in charge of the construction and
maintenance of all the school buildings in New York City,
and for several years he was president of the National Council on Schoolhouse Construction. The school buildings he
caused to be erected seemed always to have a pair of cement
lions in front, each lion holding up, under one paw, a blank
cement shield. However, when he died, his obituary in the
Times said that "he achieved nationwide recognition as an
authority on school planning."

When Mary and I were children, he always took us for a
visit to his office once a year. Even a child could see that my
father was something of a hero in the Bureau of Buildings.
The Bureau was Civil Service, but that did not keep the poli-
ticians from making occasional attempts to manipulate it to
their advantage. My father met them with bared teeth, and
they retired in unwonted confusion. Like Robespierre, he
was a pea-green incorruptible. It was part of his job to let out
contracts to various kinds of construction firms and every
Christmas some of these people, who did not know him, sent

him handsome presents. He always sent them back. A man in his position, he said, could not accept gifts.

Reinhold was the strictest toilet trainer since Bismarck and would turn white with rage if a child wet the bed, but he loved Christmas and for several days at that season Mary and I could rely absolutely on his not losing his temper, no matter what the provocation. When he was in a good mood, he wrestled with us. "Reinhold! You're too rough!" Annie would say. He was. He did not know how to temper the wind to the shorn lamb. But it was a physical contact and those, once we got past infancy, we never got from Annie.

I was terrified of my father's anger, and he turned my knees to water so often that they rose and fell with the tide. Nevertheless, I did not appease him as I did my mother. At some point after I had learned to swim, the Knights of Columbus built a clubhouse in South Yonkers with a pool which was open to nonmembers several afternoons a week. I was in seventh heaven, but Reinhold quickly brought me back to earth. He forbade me to go there. I might pick up germs. Besides, the Knights of Columbus were Catholic. I begged and pleaded, but my father was adamant.

Overnight, defiance hardened in me. The next day I went swimming anyway, firmly blocking out of my mind the thought of punishment. There were no hair dryers in those days and Reinhold, when he came home, knew from my wet hair where I had been. He took off his belt and used it across my shoulders to such purpose that the following morning they were covered with purple welts. But that afternoon I went back. The silent awe with which my mother and sister treated me, on my return, was not reassuring and when Reinhold strode into the house that night I was close to fainting at the thought of what lay ahead. To my utter incredulity, however, he merely looked at me and said nothing. He could not have had a bad conscience about the welts, because he had not seen them. Perhaps even he sometimes wanted a truce.

He being a self-made man, "practicality" was of course his favorite word, and my inability to master arithmetic made him furious. The one talent I visibly had, however, he paid no attention to. I could write. When I was in the seventh grade, we were asked one day to do an extemporaneous essay and I glanced out of the window at the sky and wrote a piece about the approach of a thunderstorm. The teacher thought it so good that she sent it in to *The Yonkers Statesman*. The *Statesman* published it, underneath a little box which said it was a remarkable piece of writing for an eleven-year-old child. For a few days I was a heroine in Lincoln Park. But not to Reinhold.

It was not that he was a Philistine. All his life he was painfully sensitive about not having had a formal education, and he never gave up trying to supply the lack. When informative books came out like H. G. Wells's *Outline of History* or Will Durant's best-selling book on philosophy, he read every word of them. But he never read novels and to him writers were people who starved in garrets and only became famous after they were dead.

Someone said to him after the thunderstorm piece was published that I ought to become a writer when I was grown up. "There's no money in it," he replied curtly, with a dismissive wave of the hand. Not the words, but the dismissive gesture, sank in. Writing was something I might do for my own pleasure, but it was not to be taken seriously.

The following year, however, an occasion arose when I had to take it seriously. Every year the D.A.R. presented a medal on graduation night to the eighth-grade pupil who had written the best essay on any subject having to do with American history, and everybody had to submit an essay. I had smiled with pleasure while I was writing my thunderstorm piece. Nature was part of my life—winter sunsets and grasshoppers in the hot summer sun describing large parabolas when one took the path across the vacant lots. But I did not want to write an essay about any aspect of American history, especially in a competition.

With what was no doubt a compulsion to fail, I selected for my subject not Abraham Lincoln, whom I loved, but Ulysses S. Grant, whose wooden impassivity bored and baffled me. I got Grant's *Memoirs* from the public library and found them inexpressibly tedious. It did not occur to me to switch to an easier topic. Even in the eighth grade, I was unable, once having put my hand to the plow, to take that hand off the plow, though I might find myself trying to open a furrow in a basketball court. The effort to get the essay down on paper almost made me sick to my stomach, but having with inordinate difficulty bundled together 800 stilted words, I turned the thing in and forgot about it.

Commencement was an important and exciting event in P.S. 21, perhaps because it was a conspicuous milestone. It was the end of intimacy. The graduates went from there to Yonkers High School, a brick horror of Victorian Gothic as large as P.S. 21 was small and located in the center of Yonkers, a two-mile trolley ride away.

For commencement the girls' mothers all made them new white dresses. Mine was of voile in what Annie conceived of as a classical style, and we bought white canvas one-strap pumps, with bumpy toes, to go with it. I felt that as the ultimate in drapery, I could easily hold my own with the Elgin Marbles. To complete the ceremonial atmosphere, my mother, on the day of the event, made a lopsided coconut layer cake and a big pitcher of lemonade for us to celebrate with when we got home.

At the exercises, we all did recitations. I had been as-

signed a passage from the Bible. It was a hortatory passage, so
it was just my style, and I rendered it in a thunderous treble.
Resuming my seat in a glow of self-satisfaction, I was scarcely
aware that somebody else had won the D.A.R. medal.

When the program was concluded, there was a swirl of
congratulations. The boys were clapped on the shoulder, the
girls were told how pretty their dresses were, and parents and
teachers milled around in a simple jollification that was like
Breughel without the codpieces. Reinhold, to be sure, did
not congratulate me and he was ominously silent on the way
home, but I was too much exhilarated to notice.

My mother put the cake on the dining room table.

" 'There was a sound of revelry by night,' " I said, hoping to be applauded for my learning.

Reinhold turned on me.

"You're rotten, Margaret Halsey, you're rotten to the
core!"

I could not believe my ears.

My sister, quicker of apprehension than I, left the room.

It seemed that Reinhold had expected me to win the
D.A.R. medal, and he went to work on my character with
the unstoppable fury of Oliver Cromwell putting dents in the
church plate. I was lazy. I was worthless. He would have
given his eye teeth to have gotten the diploma I had just
received. How could he hold up his head on the train among
the commuters in the morning when I had failed to win the
D.A.R.?

My mother took the cake into the kitchen and did not
come back.

I did not cry. I did not protest. I did what children often
do in self-defense: I pretended that no such thing was happening. At length Reinhold wore himself out and began angrily locking up the house for the night. I went to bed and
fell asleep right away. My sister was already asleep.

I did cry, actually, for two whole days after I was graduated from P.S. 21, but not because of Reinhold's outburst. I cried because I had to go on to high school and I would not see Miss Sibley any more. Lying on the porch swing and staring agonizedly in the direction of the school, I wept inexhaustibly. Annie was disgusted with this display of emotion, but for once I did not care what she thought. On the third day the resilience of youth reasserted itself and I resumed my normal activities. On the third day, also, my father took his Brownie from the closet and told me jovially to get out my diploma and put on my graduation dress and he would snap my picture.

It is one of the insoluble problems of life that children necessarily see their parents out of context. To me, Reinhold was the Thunderer, and that was all. Being a child, I could not ask the question which would have occurred to any observant adult—namely, how did a man so extremely intelligent come to make such a marriage, with all its built-in frustrations?

The answer probably was that my father worked so hard, from his twelfth year onward, that as a young man he never had time for any social life. Hence, when he was courting Annie, he was totally inexperienced and mistook her silences for sympathy—still water running deep, and so on. A woman with vitality and a sense of humor might well have been tolerably happy with Reinhold. But poor Annie would have found a boy soprano coarse and brutish in his merciless masculinity. She needed an employer, not a husband.

The tragedy of my parents' misalliance was beyond my ken, but as a child living in the ambience of that marriage I had a feeling—nothing like a resolute determination, but just a somewhat cheerful feeling—that when I was grown up, it was not going to be like that for me.

Nor was it.

2
Within a Budding Grove

There are some who say that the only answer to man's dilemma on this planet today is decentralization. Modern technological society—with its multinational corporations, its huge and all-embracing federal governments and its mass communications—will have to go. It will have to be replaced, some people say, by a social structure divided into much smaller units, where government, education and industry are conducted on so modest a scale that the individual, *qua* individual, can participate in them and thus have some sense of controlling his own destiny.

If any such communelike units take the place of today's giganticism, childhood and youth will be quite different from what they are now. The child's or young person's knowledge of the world will unfold slowly, instead of arriving *tout complèt* in the living room via the television screen. Some of this knowledge of the world may be inaccurate, but not irreversibly so.

In my generation, in provincial America, we were still far enough away from giganticism for knowledge of the world to unfold slowly. For me, both high school and college were an experience of slowly dissolving ignorance, and I got out of that experience a sense of gradually expanding personal

46

power which is denied to the young person sitting in front of television and watching two men who look like ruptured polar bears walking on the moon.

Lest it seem that I am indulging in futile nostalgia, let it be said at once that the City of Yonkers in 1922 was extremely badly run, politically, with the result that Yonkers High School was obsolete, ill-equipped and painfully overcrowded. Nevertheless, for a graduate of secluded and homogeneous P.S. 21, it was an illuminating place. Yonkers was a factory town and there were a lot of pupils in Yonkers High with names like Di Salvo and Schawinsky. There were also well-to-do Anglo-Saxons of purest ray serene from Park Hill. Neither sort of person had I ever come into contact with before.

Because of having been skipped in grammar school, I was much younger than the other freshmen. The other girls were wearing flowered print dresses and shoes with Cuban heels, and I was still in middies and skirts and black cotton stockings. Also, I was a head shorter than they. I was not aware of being unhappy about it. Twelve-year-olds in those days were not expected to bemoan their lot, and Yonkers High was in very truth illuminating. Without intending to, it furnished intimations that life was more complicated, and good and evil less instantly and definitively separable, than existence in Lincoln Park had led one to suppose.

In one of my classes there was a girl named Maeve Gilbey who was much older than the other students. Maeve Gilbey was beautiful. Her hair was of cornsilk gold and she had fine, delicate skin, good features and a gentle, tranquil, dreamy manner. That, at least, was the way I interpreted it. She may have been just lethargic. Maeve was casual in her attendance. She never carried books, never took notes, never did any homework, and when called upon in class admitted with a seraphic smile that she did not know the answer.

Though I was a rank outsider, I could listen, and I heard the other girls saying in shocked tones that Maeve Gilbey went out with older men. Not college boys—who, heaven knows, were the pinnacle of worldly sophistication—but men as old as your father.

This could have but one meaning.

"She's no better than she should be."

They were dread words. Sometimes the grown-ups said them, and I always had a pang of terror at the scornful dismissal in their voices. Would those words ever be said of me? I was not really sure how to prevent it. Surreptitiously—and in heart-pounding fear of being caught—I had looked up "fornication" in the dictionary after I encountered it in the Bible. "Illicit sexual intercourse," the dictionary said, which left me no further ahead than I was before.

The mechanics of sexual congress were completely unknown to me, but in those remote, pre-media days there was a kind of knowledge that sifted down on you from the leaves of the trees, emanated from the fronts of the houses you walked past and got into you through the soles of your feet as you trod the sidewalks. From this sort of instruction I had learned that a lady finds whatever it is that men and women do together distasteful, and that when this whatever-it-is takes place between two people who are not married to each other, the female partner, though not the male, is irretrievably declassed.

But Maeve Gilbey was clearly not declassed—at least, not *my* idea of declassed. From the trees, the house fronts and the sidewalks I had learned that once a woman has "illicit sexual intercourse" she develops an insatiable appetite for it, and this appetite very quickly makes her raddled, red-eyed and brassy-voiced. Maeve, however—though there was no doubt in my mind that she was a fallen woman—looked like a Christmas angel and behaved like one. She disappeared at the end of the year, but while she was there, she fascinated me. I could not keep my eyes off her, and was disappointed on the days when she failed to show up in class.

In another of my classes there was a boy who was also much older than the rest of the students and who, like Maeve Gilbey, challenged one's implanted beliefs. He was called Hobart Krale and he was Jewish. Hobart Krale (Hobart! delightful name!) was handsome, and he did not look the way I thought all Jews looked. Nor did he act the way I thought all Jews acted.

Far from being a bespectacled grind, he seemed to share with Maeve Gilbey the attitude that Yonkers High was a negligible institution. He laughed a great deal, had an easy manner and told jokes, and the d'Artagnan effect of casual daring was reinforced by the fact that he wore a raccoon coat—supposedly the earmark of college men. A cooler-headed observer might have thought that if Hobart Krale, at his age, was only a freshman in high school, he must be a bubble-headed wastrel, but I was incapable of such vinegary skepticism.

The Prohibition Amendment was still in effect at that time and there was a great deal of news in the papers about gangsters. Hobart Krale's father was said to be mixed up with gangsters, and this rumor was forcibly substantiated one day when Mr. Krale was murdered. The Krale family moved away immediately, but I thought about Hobart for a long time afterward. Was he still laughing and making jokes? I could not imagine him bereaved.

Since I was so visibly a fugitive from the bassinet, I did not have what was later called a peer group, and to fill the void, I turned to religion. There was a big Episcopal church near the high school, and I started going to church on weekdays as well as Sunday. My parents' marriage had by this time settled into a tense and silent hatred that was almost mechanical, but since they had children to bring up, they could not help but find occasional points of unity. One such common ground was that they were both taken aback by my churchgoing. Ostensibly believers in the Christian virtues, the god they really worshiped was Respectability and the last thing they wanted was anyone in the family with a religious vocation.

They need not have worried. I went to church because it gave me a sense of belonging and perhaps also because the church was spacious and vaulted, whereas both the place where I lived and the place where I went to school were cramped. And eventually the candle-lit pageant of Episcopalianism wore thin. It was humanity, not divinity, I was in quest of, albeit an idealized humanity, and in my sophomore year I found it in the movies.

My appetite for the movies became voracious the minute I discovered them. In their luxurious darkness and privacy I sat transfixed by the action bodied forth on a screen not much larger than my mother's best tablecloth and by the subtitles which explained it.

"Came the dawn."

"Meanwhile, back at the ranch . . ."

"We'll cut them off at the pass."

And the stars themselves—Conrad Nagel, Billie Dove, Richard Dix (my favorite), Pauline Frederick, Renée Adorée, the Gish sisters, Corinne Griffith, Constance Bennett, Douglas Fairbanks, John Gilbert and Ramon Navarro. There were giants in the earth in those days. Or so it seemed to me.

I might have been better employed. Sophomore year I had an English teacher named Miss Simon, who was Jewish. It was agreed by the students—who spoke of her with respect but not with warmth—that Miss Simon was "good," and one day she asked me to stay after the others left. When I was alone with her, she spoke with what seemed to me preternatural solemnity.

"You can write," she said.

Conventionally, I ought to report that my face lit up, that I started pouring out to her all my dreams of becoming a famous author when I grew up, and that I shyly confessed to spending hours scribbling in a ten-cent-store notebook. But what stood in front of Miss Simon, in Ground Gripper shoes and "sensible" clothes, was the Sealed Mind of the Halseys.

Reinhold had spoken. Writing was an exciting part of being "good in English," but nothing more. I was always glad when the teachers gave us book reports or themes to do. It was my favorite kind of homework. But it never occurred to me to do any writing that was not assigned, and far from being kindled and rapturous about what Miss Simon had said, I was merely puzzled that she seemed to think she was telling me something very important. Perhaps it was some mysterious aspect of her Jewishness? It must have been an odd experience for Miss Simon—to discover what seemed like talent and evoke from the owner, when the good news was imparted, only a blank stare.

While I was still living in the phantom world of the movies, reality started to intrude in a way that was impossible to ignore. I commenced to mature physically. I grew much taller and began to develop breasts. They embarrassed me keenly—they were so pointy!—and though both parents had always hammered away at the importance of standing up straight, I stooped as much as possible in order to minimize them. Fledgling though they were, they loomed in my mind like the foothills of the Adirondacks.

Annie took official cognizance of their appearance by saying one day, in a veritable paroxysm of self-consciousness, that she guessed she would have to get me a Ferris waist.

"No!" I said explosively.

A Ferris waist was a sort of corselet which went from armpit to crotch and into which some mothers, but not all, put their pubescent daughters. The brassiere was beginning to displace the Ferris waist, but not in Lincoln Park. At any rate, I reacted violently against the idea of any such constriction, and Annie was overjoyed to let the subject drop.

When things changed, they changed fast. The last two years of high school were as different from the first as a rose garden from an Arctic tundra. Among the non-working-class young people—who, in their own eyes and in mine, were the only ones who counted—the social life of Yonkers High had two foci, North and South Yonkers. At the beginning of junior year, I was discovered and accepted by the South Yonkers coterie. It was unbelievable. The age gap was closed. I was asked for dates. I went to dances and basketball games and the movies.

Bliss was it in that dawn to be alive. To be sure, homework and household tasks went on as usual, and there was no letup in my self-appointed task of placating and seeking the approval of every grown-up in sight—parents, teachers, neighbors and even streetcar conductors. Nevertheless, I lived in a state of carbonated euphoria.

I was astonished at how easy it was to learn the ropes. Nobody had to tell me that when a popular girl went out with a drip, the girl did not raise the drip to her level. The drip pulled the girl down to his. I knew by instinct how far you could go with the verbal clowning which passed in that circle for wit and I automatically suppressed what would be disturbing. God, for instance, was not mocked. Nor were marriage, motherhood, protective tariffs or going to college in order to "make contacts."

At that time, the most damning word in my mother's vocabulary was "boy-crazy." Nothing brought out the Lady

Prioress in her more strongly than the suggestion that "a young girl"—she put a world of ominous meaning into the phrase—might feel attracted to the opposite sex. As a matter of fact, no girl ever went through Yonkers High School who was more boy-crazy than I, but Annie never used the word about me. Absorbed in her domestic treadmill, she was oblivious to the pagan raptures seething beneath my well-behaved exterior.

But the pagan raptures were there. The high school dances were usually held in the gymnasium of the Y.W.C.A., and when some boy I had a crush on came into the room, it always seemed to me that the light changed. I was no longer seeing the objects about me through the agency of electric current coursing through insulated wires. Instead the balloons, the crepe-paper streamers, the gym equipment, the stag line and the orchestra were suddenly bathed in the kind of celestial lambency which the Old Masters portrayed in pictures of the Annunciation. Since there was always some boy I had a crush on, I must have saved the Y.W.C.A. quite a lot of money on its light bills.

When my sister reached the age to have dates, she took no interest in boys nor they in her. She went around with a covey of girls who were as boyless as herself. Except for my sister, who continued to be low-keyed, Mary's friends were very jolly and had funny names for each other like "Bitsey" and "Muffy." My mother approved heartily of these celibates and called them "wholesome." The very word made me shudder.

Though my translation from runt of the litter to girl-about-South-Yonkers seemed to me as miraculous as Lazarus being raised from the dead, it was actually owing at least in part to "progress." While I was busy playing hide and seek in Lincoln Park, some kind soul had thoughtfully perfected the self-starter. The automobile had become common enough so that a high school boy could count on being allowed to have the family car on a reasonable number of Saturday nights. Lincoln Park was thus drawn into the orbit of South Yonkers and a girl who lived there was not too inaccessible to be asked for a date.

"Progress" was a word that was on everyone's lips in the mid-1920s, but compared to the pace it developed later, it was halting. Our families were gradually acquiring gadgets—vacuum cleaners, washing machines with wringers on top—but there were no power mowers or electric hedge clippers and boys were expected to mow lawns and trim hedges with their not-yet-obsolete muscles. Sleek Scandinavian furniture was far off in the future, and our tables, sideboards and cabinets ran a good deal to rosettes and curlicues. You did not polish that furniture with a mere flick of the wrist, after spraying it with wax from a pressurized container. You put lemon oil on it and rubbed all those bumps and excrescences until the cloth dropped from your paralyzed hand.

We knew about vitamins, but they did not come in pill form. You had to get them the toilsome way, by eating vegetables. We were also very germ-conscious, and people still remembered the terrible Spanish influenza epidemic of 1918 as a kind of Slaughter of the Innocents. But Kleenex had still to appear on the market and when we had colds, we carried about in our pockets handkerchiefs that only a pathologist could love.

The permanent wave had not yet been invented, though it was just around the corner. My hair was thin and fine and uncompromisingly straight and America's imagination had been captured—apparently forever—by Mary Pickford's curls, so I went every week to have a marcel wave. The marcel wave made one appear to have been roofed with a bit of corrugated iron, but I thought those small, geometrically rigid scallops enchanting. The great drawback of the marcel, however, was its vulnerability. You had merely to step out on the porch on a rainy night and the wave uncurled like a striking rattlesnake.

Nevertheless, I had one advantage which I failed to appreciate. Neither I nor anyone else I was able to observe had to go through the ordeal of acne, blackheads and skin eruptions that often seem to afflict the young of a more developed economy. Not that South Yonkers was Arcadia, or that we all looked pink and white and unblemished like Staffordshire shepherds and shepherdesses. We had the occasional pimple, but circumstances did not favor the overactive sebaceous gland. There were no Good Humor men, nor did vending machines make Coke and packaged potato chips instantly available.

But what we gained on epidermis, we lost on teeth. Nobody in those days had orthodontia and there were a lot of citizens around whose bite was worse than their bark. The people pictured in advertisements generally had their mouths closed and when it came to pretty or ugly teeth, one took what the Deity had handed out and perforce lived with it. Reinhold—who in my view had done nothing else for me—had at least passed on his teeth, which were creditable, and on rainy nights when I had a date my face was wreathed in one continuous, nonstop smile which I hoped would distract attention from the havoc that had overtaken my marcel wave.

Much of America at that time was engaged in a frenzy of stock market speculation and the Prohibition Amendment was widely flouted. Indeed, one or two highly respectable families in Yonkers were suspected of having a finger in the bootlegging pie. But though F. Scott Fitzgerald was writing about the dissipations of the rich, we never did anything in our crowd that could not have been safely pictured in a Norman Rockwell cover for *The Saturday Evening Post*.

We were neither sensitive nor idealistic, we young people. We never stopped for a minute to wonder what our classmates whose fathers worked in the factories did for recreation, and we reveled in all the standard prejudices of the Calvin Coolidge era against Jews, Negroes, Catholics and the foreign-born. But we were principled as we understood principle. Cheating on exams was *mal vu*, and stealing or the slightest dishonesty about money would have put one beyond the pale. And we had one great advantage which has been denied to more enlightened generations. We were not a teenage market, so we were able to mature in privacy.

It was my belief that I had broken completely free in spirit from my stuffy family, but though I knew the ropes and was endlessly delighted by the sense of belonging, I formed no close friendships and this was no doubt due to Annie's subterranean influence. There was also, merely in the way my father lived, an implied criticism of the South Yonkers families whose ideas and attitudes, as represented by their adolescent children, I so joyously and uncritically accepted. Most of the fathers of the boys who took me out had been to college, though some of them had had to work their way through. Even these latter my father was jealous of, as having had more opportunities than he. And he certainly could have made better use of a college education.

He subscribed to *The Atlantic* and not *The Saturday Evening Post*. On Sundays and holidays he sometimes went in to the city to the Metropolitan Museum or the Museum of Natural History, though nobody else ever stirred out of Yonkers, save to go to New York to work or shop and, once a year, to a musical comedy. Reinhold occasionally bought books. I recall his bringing home Walter Lippmann's *A Preface to Morals*. In the boys' households where I was sometimes asked to Sunday dinner, the library never consisted of more than half a dozen books and they were Westerns by authors, household words in their day, whose names would now be known only to oldsters: Zane Grey and Harold Bell Wright.

But whatever subterranean influence my parents might have had, I was quite unaware of. What was in the forefront of my consciousness, those last two years in high school, was the way Reinhold behaved about my going out with boys. My first few dates he did not seem to notice. Then, one Friday night, when I had bolted my dinner and was just about to rush off and get dressed, his voice stopped me.

"What do you think you're doing?"

The sheer livid menace that an old-fashioned parent could pack into that phrase would have stopped a battalion of tanks.

"I have a date," I said, and the mere saying of it was so new and so exhilarating that for a moment I expected him to catch the contagion of my excitement and rejoice with me. But the answering voice was pure whiplash.

"You have no such thing. I won't have you running around with boys."

This last was a phrase my mother used to describe girls who were not "wholesome," so I knew he had been querying her. He had not been inattentive. He had merely been lying in wait.

"But *everybody* does!"

Not being one to calculate or look ahead, I had not stopped to think, when boys started paying attention to me, that the cup might be dashed from my lips, though experience should have taught me that dashing cups from lips was the way Victorian parents got most of their exercise.

"You're not everybody. Get on the phone and tell that boy you can't go."

Annie got up quickly and began closing windows. Mary looked from our father to me with a detached curiosity.

"But I *can't!* What would he *think?*"

I could see myself at the front door downstairs—we lived upstairs at the time—meeting my date with swollen, tear-stained face and telling him in a choked voice that my father would not let me go out. All too well I could visualize his surprise and embarrassment. He would never telephone me again. Neither would any other boy. And what about going to school on Monday? It would be like turning up without warning hideously disfigured.

"It's too late," I said, in a storm of tears. "He can't get another date now."

"That's his problem."

Mary, looking bored, got up from the table and left the room. Her going made me suddenly aware of the dining room furniture crowding in on us—sideboard, china closet and serving table leaving barely room for the chairs to be pushed back from the dining table. To spend this and every other Friday and Saturday evening at home, while the others held hands in the movies . . .

The deprivation was unendurable.

"But why not?"

There was a portentous silence and then Reinhold spoke.

"I work."

Another majestic pause.

"I need my sleep," he said. "I can't stay awake half the night wondering where you are."

"But we're only going to the movies!"

I was trembling with helpless rage at my father's hypocrisy. The pious incantation about work did not conceal for a moment his Puritan zest for denying, withholding and punishing.

Annie intervened.

"Reinhold," she said. "I trust Margaret."

I sensed instantly that she was role-playing. She was being the mother of a well-brought-up girl. There would be no real help from that quarter.

"You let me go last week," I challenged my father.

I could see from his face that this argument registered. The next moment, however, his features took on the studied blankness of one who is going to ignore a reasonable statement because he is in a position to do so.

"You're not in school to go gadding about. You stay home and study."

"But I've done my homework!"

I was almost suffocated with despair. How could my parents dismiss contemptuously as "running around with boys" what to me, after the isolation of freshman and sophomore years, was nothing less than heaven?

"You're only fourteen," thundered Reinhold.

"That's not my fault! I didn't ask to be skipped in school."

Again the point registered, and he seemed close to conceding it, but Annie cut in.

"Reinhold! Margaret! Keep your voices down. Do you want the neighbors to hear?"

Both my father and I were far beyond thought of the neighbors. I pleaded my cause frantically, reiterating that everybody did it, that my marks were good, that he hadn't any *reason* . . .

I pleaded the more frantically because of a sense of something huge and ominous left unstated. Victorian prudery kept my father from saying what was in his mind— namely, that these boys I wanted to go out with were idle libertines scheming to debauch me. Concupiscence, however, was as far outside my frame of reference as embezzlement or simony. Lacking intimates, I still did not know how sexual union was achieved. Nevertheless, some kind of accusation was apparently being leveled in a tacit way against both the boys and me, and I could not come to grips with it because it was too shadowy.

There was no time to reflect on such intangibles, however, for my father was enumerating for the thousandth time the many advantages I enjoyed which he had not, and which presumably gave him the right to expect unquestioning submission from me.

"I didn't ask to be born!" I shrieked, maddened by this graceless, heavy-handed demand for gratitude.

"Neither did I," he said bitterly, which brought me up short for an instant, as it had not occurred to me there was *anything* my father could not control if he wanted to.

Annie, I could tell from her frown, was getting impatient. She wanted me to give in. Then she would have not only immediate peace but also material for months and years of spiteful remarks, fervently subscribed to by me, about Reinhold's overbearingness.

My father and I, however, were inexhaustible.

"Who *is* this boy?" demanded Reinhold, and later, in a stentorian voice, "How will I know what you're doing?"

When I said I would run away from home, Reinhold laughed harshly. A minute later he said that if I did not get to that phone, he would call the boy himself.

"You can't," I said viciously. "You don't know his name."

Even as I spoke, I knew I had made a disastrous tactical error. Reinhold had no tolerance whatsoever for taunts from schoolgirls, and he might respond to this one by carrying me bodily to my room, locking me in and answering the bell himself when my date came. Luckily for me, however, my father was pompous even in his rages, and he had already started to tell me the story of his life.

Revolutions, we had been taught in my sophomore history course, do not occur simply because people are down-trodden. Revolutions, the history teacher said, occur when people have gained a little freedom and their masters then try to take it away from them. Between one moment and the next, I became a revolutionary. I would kill Reinhold, or force him to kill me, but no power on earth was going to make me go to Yonkers High School and be a girl who did not have dates.

Did this sudden implacability in some way com-municate itself to Reinhold? Could he see it in my face? At any rate, he switched abruptly to the subject of my defects of character, and after calling me lazy, selfish, weak and rotten spoiled, he said in a transport of rage, "I wash my hands of you!" and strode out of the room.

My tears dried instantly. Buoyant with relief and happi-ness, and without even a glance at Annie, I raced off to get dressed.

Strange to say, not once during all those two years did Reinhold actually stop me from going out on a date, al-though we had a battle to the death every weekend. My sis-ter, that cool hand, would casually have defied him and there would have been an end to it, but I was what Annie called "high-strung," which was no doubt what impelled Reinhold to embark on a policy of harassment.

At one time, he said that I could only go out with boys whose fathers he knew. This was tantamount to my not going out at all, because the fathers of the South Yonkers boys commuted to New York on the main-line train which ran along the Hudson River, whereas Reinhold took the little spur line which went through Lincoln Park.

At another time he said I could go out, but I must be back by ten thirty. I reacted like a patient being operated on without an anesthetic, for such a limitation would have left no time to go to the little restaurant we all frequented after

the movies and basketball games. Reinhold said if I wanted
a sandwich, I could bring the boy home and get one. His intellectual honesty saved me that time. Seeing the look on my
face, he gave an enormous clearing of the throat which signaled a retreat from his position. He knew as well as I did how
my mother would respond to having a stranger lounging
about "her" kitchen. A boy I had never been out with before
had to come upstairs and be introduced to my family—Annie
understood that convention was inflexible on that point—but
after that I met them at the front door.

One ill-fated day the Mayor of Yonkers said in a newspaper interview that he would never let a daughter of his go
out in a car with a young man. His Honor was childless and
I had often heard my father describe him as a corrupt, small-
time politician, but with this statement he suddenly became
to Reinhold a Dr. Spock. The decree was laid down: I could
only go out with a boy if we went on the trolley. It took a bit
of doing, that night, to bring Reinhold to the point where he
washed his hands of me.

But one ultimate piece of harassment I did not argue
with him about. The first Friday that my father had said he
would not have me running around with boys, I came happily home to behold a sight that froze me. There at the top of
the stairs sat Reinhold, in bathrobe and slippers, pale as he
always was when beside himself with anger, and with a po-
liceman's nightstick laid across his lap. He had gotten the
nightstick years before, after we heard the mysterious noise in
the cellar, and it always hung by its leather thong next to the
mirror in his bedroom.

I supposed he intended to beat me up. He said nothing
and from my angle of vision at the bottom of the stairs, he
appeared about eight feet tall. All the menace in the world
seemed to be comprised in that towering, silent figure. I
could not turn and flee the house. There was no place to go.

Panic blurred my vision and my knees threatened to buckle beneath me, but I knew that the challenge had to be taken up. I had to get up the stairs and walk past my father as if I had not observed anything out of the way. It was like going down the Last Mile to the execution chamber at Sing Sing, but somehow I managed to do it and gain the safety of the bedroom, where Mary was alseep.

Almost every time I had a date, those last two years in high school, I came home to find Reinhold with the night-stick at the top of the stairs, and every single time I was as paralyzed with fright as I had been the first time. Neither my father nor I ever spoke, and though my mother must have known about this little tableau, she never mentioned it. It was just a silent, terrible ordeal that was the price of going out with boys, and except for the moments when it was actually happening, I did not think of it.

The now-forgotten Alexander Woollcott once referred to "catching life in the act of rhyming," and Reinhold's night-stick performance was a perfect example of it. The very instrument my father employed to intimidate me was what steeled me to resistance, because it reminded me of the time when I was a small child and had seen my father forcing himself to do something he was afraid to do. Without Reinhold's own example, I would never in the world have been able, weekend after weekend, to mount those stairs and walk past him into the bedroom. He had builded better than he knew.

3

To Horse and Away!

I have a B.S. degree from Skidmore College, in Saratoga Springs, New York, in something called Secretarial Science, and a Master's degree in English from Teachers College, Columbia University, and that is just about the least amount of education you can get for the money. In the 1920s, the phrase "personnel work" was just beginning to be used, and my father's plan for my future was that I should be the first woman personnel manager of a bank—a career which seemed to him to combine the maximum of distinction with the maximum of safety.

Skidmore was primarily a liberal arts school, but it also gave degrees in Nursing, Home Economics and a gruesome collection of courses in Statistics, Business Law and Commercial Geography lumped under the title of Secretarial Science. In this last Reinhold enrolled me, much to my dismay. But my father said it was either that, or not going to college at all. Characteristically, in his plan to make a lady banker out of me, he was attempting to ride roughshod over an insuperable obstacle, which was that I was so bad in mathematics that when I was in Yonkers High, I had had to take Intermediate Algebra three times before I passed it.

Actually, in my second week at Skidmore I did learn something about personnel work, though it was not quite the sort that my father had had in mind. Browsing in the library one afternoon, I came across a pamphlet by a woman named Mary Ware Dennett which had been written to explain sexual intercourse to children. By today's standards the pamphlet would seem as innocuous as a Methodist hymnal, but Mrs. Dennett had, in that darker era, been haled into court for publishing it. I was sixteen, and I emerged from the library into the glorious autumn weather of upper New York State with the sense that there was nothing more in the world I needed to know.

But there *was* more.

Three teachers at Skidmore awakened me to what is now called social consciousness. They were the head of the English Department, Dr. Bolton; his wife, who also taught English; and Mr. Cheney, who was in himself the whole Economics Department. Cheney—as he was always called— was an odd little man, socially rather gauche, but principled and stubbornly independent. He regularly ran for office on the Socialist ticket, which in Saratoga Springs took courage. The townspeople said that Cheney had been bought by Moscow gold and periodically pressured the college to get rid of him.

Unlike Cheney, who was the acquired taste of a very few students, the Boltons were admired by everyone. They were young and lighthearted. Mrs. Bolton was mocking and delicately ironic, and her husband was a natural-born enthusiast whose communication was rendered delightful by a kind of pixie humor. Perhaps because he was something of a biblical scholar, Dr. Bolton was a fervent Zionist, though this was twenty years before the formation of the State of Israel, and he used to lecture on the subject in the towns and villages nearby. It was not a topic which laid them in the aisles in rural New York State, but Dr. Bolton had charm and he was in demand oftener than one would think.

Sometimes life itself force-feeds one. When my sister and I were children, anti-Semitism was an integral part of our existence. Somebody once said that thinking is hard work, but prejudice is a pleasure. It certainly was. Making anti-Semitic remarks gave one a sense of effortless superiority unobtainable in any other way. But when I got to Skidmore, Cheney and the Boltons quite unwittingly offered a different and a much less fleeting pleasure—that of being with people whose impulses were generous and whose imaginations extended beyond the spiky stockade of self. Observing, to my initial surprise, that my new mentors strongly disapproved of anti-Semitism, I abandoned it immediately.

The Boltons were warmly hospitable and the students they regarded as interesting were much at their house. But Mrs. Bolton beneath her mockery was a strongly maternal woman, and we Brighties had to share her attention with various birds-with-broken-wings who had touched her ready sympathy. That, too, was part of the force-feeding. The Boltons were unpunctual, improvident and unworldly, and no doubt they had trouble spots in their marriage or with their two children, as everybody does. I, however, was too inexperienced to recognize any problem less starkly visible than a harelip or a broken leg, and to me they were happy, romantic figures for whom I would have laid down my life.

The sacrifice would have been worth it if for no other reason than that their laughter was so easily evoked. At home I had learned to suppress any quips that rose to mind because my mother and sister reacted to them like the National Congress of Public Executioners. With the advantage of hindsight, I now think that laughter grated on their basic despair, but at the time I knew only that at any extravagant simile of mine, my sister would address herself to some imaginary person standing behind me and say, "That Margaret. She thinks she's so smart." Annie—though it was not the locution she would have used herself—did not demur. The Boltons, on the other hand, being witty themselves, created an atmosphere which brought out wit in others.

Luckily, the Secretarial Science course permitted a fair number of electives, and I took all the courses I could with either Cheney or the Boltons. I also wrote sonnets which were very obviously derived from Edna St. Vincent Millay and had a humorous column in the college newspaper. At that time Franklin P. Adams had a column, very famous in its day, in *The New York World* and once a week he printed contributions from readers. Urged on by the Boltons, I sent in several items and he used two or three of them.

But writing for me was still a matter of being "good in English." I knew I had to get a secretarial job as soon as I finished school, and I had no wish to hole up in an attic somewhere and spend all my evenings and weekends writing. When told that I ought to become a professional writer, I always replied that I had nothing to say. It was a truthful answer. Even the Boltons had had only a minimal effect on the Sealed Mind of the Halseys, and like a corpse in a glacier, I had rosy cheeks, but I was not traveling very fast.

I thought I was traveling fast, however. The Prohibition Amendment was still in force and college boys at dances carried flasks in their hip pockets and boasted obsessively about their drinking. The Girl in the Glacier did not drink, fearing above all things loss of control, but I accepted the college boys at their own valuation as boldly defiant rebels against Puritanism. Politically, in particular, I thought myself highly emancipated. Very few Skidmore girls in the Class of 1930 took any interest in politics, but in Cheney's little coterie we were articulate champions of free trade, Al Smith, trade unions, Sacco and Vanzetti and the League of Nations.

We were also fervent disciples of H. L. Mencken, who, we felt, was leading us out of the land of Egypt, out of the house of bondage.

For my own part, I was aware that I was being educated—though not, because of the time demanded by Secretarial Science, to the kind of erudition which would enable a person to spit in the eye of Simone de Beauvoir. What I did not realize was that I was accepting the education only up to a point. Cheney and Dr. Bolton both put their convictions into practice, even though it meant swimming against the stream. I, on the other hand, thought that merely entertaining humanitarian ideas was enough. Despite my theoretical egalitarianism, I wore fraternity pins and never dreamed of criticizing the snobbery and cruel exclusiveness of the fraternity system. In fact, I liked it.

To the Kent State generations, college in the 1920s must seem like four years in a playpen. In October of my senior year the stock market crashed and the Depression was upon us, but there were few immediate effects at Skidmore. Annie came up for my graduation, but Reinhold stayed at home. I was graduated tenth in a class of one hundred and ten, and my father sent a message—or so Annie said—that this was such a poor scholastic showing that he did not think it worthwhile to make the trip.

My father had given up the nightstick routine once I got into college, but I had told the Boltons he was a monster and assured them with equal fervor that my mother was a saint. When Annie came up for graduation, Mrs. Bolton had her for tea and carefully made no comment afterward—an omission I did not notice. My mother had only one comment on Mrs. Bolton. I was a familar in the Boltons' house and at some point or other, Annie and I happened to be standing alone on their back porch, where Mrs. Bolton kept a large earthen crock full of stuffed olives. The Boltons' little boy, who was about three or four, came out and, plunging both hands into the crock, started gorging himself on stuffed olives.

"Mark my words," said Annie, "that child will never grow to manhood."

(He did, however, and turned out to have inherited his father's leprechaunish humor.)

Graduation was the end of the Skidmore playpen. Reinhold had pulled strings and gotten me a job in a small bank in downtown Manhattan. I hated the bank from the moment I set foot in it, though I was, despite my inexperience, secretary to the vice-president who really ran the place. The vice-president had not himself been to college, and he wanted a secretary who had a degree. His name was Felix Raven, and never was "Felix" used more inappropriately. A bachelor with one of Those Mothers, Mr. Raven was a driving, humorless battering ram who was considered very young to have gotten as far as he had. But he did not look young, and although bankers were traditionally supposed to be suave, Felix had the manners of a husky at feeding time.

Nevertheless, I did my job conscientiously and with great attention to detail, and after a while Felix indicated that he was not displeased by suggesting—like one proposing a delicious treat—that I should go to night school at the bank's expense and take some courses in banking. Concealing my dismay, I temporized. Banking to Mr. Raven was wife, mistress, houri and Bunny Girl, but to me it was just another Ferris waist.

The seemingly lucky circumstance of a friend's getting me another job at five dollars more a week saved me from the embarrassment of an outright "No" on the banking courses. I left the bank to become a dictaphone operator in the office of a big real estate management company, and it was very quickly evident that I had not bettered myself, despite the extra money. I worked in the Inspection and Maintenance Department, sitting with three other girls in the back of a large room filled with engineers where, with earphones on our heads from nine to five, we typed out the engineers' reports on assorted architecture. I was good at it, because Reinhold was an architect and I knew the terminology, but it was monotonous and depressing to a degree.

"Every time I think I've touched bottom as far as boredom is concerned," I wrote to the Boltons, "new vistas of ennui open up."

However, I was immobilized, because the Depression rolled inexorably on and although I tried to write to the Boltons entertainingly, I lived from month to month in ever-deepening despair—the intense, high-octane-fueled despair of youth, unmitigated by perspective. Ph.D.s from the Harvard School of Business were on their knees begging for the chance to empty wastebaskets, so how likely was it that I would find a way out of this bleak cul-de-sac? We did not know in those days that the hydrogen bomb was going to come along, and the Depression seemed like the end of the world.

All through my obedient early years, I had looked forward to being grown up, when I would have freedom and power; and then maturity, when it finally arrived, was a worse prison than childhood. There appeared to be nothing ahead except spending the rest of my life being a dictaphone operator for a real estate company. After Cheney and the Boltons, the people in South Yonkers who had once so delighted me seemed wearisome and hopelessly limited. Marriage was no way out of either the job or living at home with my parents because in those days young men thought they had to have financial prospects in order to marry and none of the young men had them.

I reacted to the despair by going to sleep. Every night when I got home, I had dinner; washed the white collar and cuffs which, as an early-Rosalind-Russell female employee, I wore on my dark dress; and went to bed, where I was asleep the minute I lay down; and I slept away most of the weekend. People did not take pills and drugs in those days and there was, of course, no television. You had to generate your own sedation.

Compared to the bomb-cratered history of more recent years, the Depression seems a mere dimple of misery, but it contained germs of future disaster that we were not aware of at the time. I took the economic debacle as simply my own personal tragedy; but others, less provincial and self-centered, were moved by the undeserved suffering they saw at every hand to turn hopeful eyes to Russia. The Soviet government was still an experiment rather than an Establishment, and it seemed logical to think that a state-planned economy was the answer to economic chaos.

Some of these people joined the Communist Party. Others expressed great sympathy with it. They were soon disillusioned. Political purges in Moscow and manipulated famine in the Volga produced undeserved suffering, too— suffering far worse than any engendered by the Depression. But fifteen or twenty years later, after World War II, the long-defunct Communist affiliations which had been momentarily inspired by the Depression were used with deadly effect by the McCarthyites.

Mercifully, we could not in the early 1930s foresee the future. The present seemed bad enough. And against the present I eventually rebelled. Blindly. I had been at the real estate company for about a year when, sitting at my dictaphone one day, it came to me between one moment and the next that if I did not get out of that place immediately, all the rest of my life would be ruined. So I walked into the office manager's lair and told him I was leaving at the end of the week.

To leave a job in the middle of the Depression was certifiable lunacy and when, that evening, I had to tell my father what I had done, my voice literally squeaked with fright. But to my measureless astonishment, Reinhold merely gave me a long stare and then barked out that I had better hump myself and get another job right away, because he wasn't going to have me lopping around the house doing nothing.

With all the odds against it, I was employed again within three weeks. A college friend got me a job with a man named Tom Stix who was a radio agent. Mr. Stix worked at home, and he and his wife very soon took me into their family. I ate meals with them, ran errands for them, and sometimes stayed the night in their apartment. In the summer I took their children to Martha's Vineyard.

The Stix clients were well-known people, though time has silted over some of them since. Franklin P. Adams, Hendrik van Loon, the actress Miriam Hopkins, John Gunther and James Thurber were the kind of personalities who came to the house. I was only the secretary in the background, and much too diffident to call attention to myself, but after the bank, the real estate company and the spiritual igloo that was my family's house, life once again seemed full of excitement, interest and human warmth.

In this atmosphere, so much more civilized than the fraternity-house revels of Skidmore days, I allowed my employer to introduce me to alcohol. At the end of every day, before I made the long trip back to Yonkers, he and I had two cocktails, and I made the happy discovery that I had a good head for liquor and that it gave me a self-confidence I had never had before.

The daily cocktails were fun, but on a more serious occasion Mr. Stix held me up to a standard of civilized behavior when I would otherwise have lapsed from it. During the bank and dictaphone period I had drifted into being semi-engaged to a young man in South Yonkers. I was a far from enraptured fiancée, for we had nothing in common beyond the fact that we had been through Yonkers High School together, but it seemed the only chance—and even at that a remote one—of getting away from my parents. Since I had two legs on the trophy for Most Self-Absorbed Girl on the Eastern Seaboard, it did not occur to me that I was using a sentient human being with no regard for his needs but solely to provide for my own.

One day I said casually to Mr. Stix that I was going to write the young man a letter and break the engagement.

"You can't write him a letter," said Mr. Stix. "You must tell him in person."

I gave him a sick look, but I knew he was right. It was a shattering interview. The young man was angry and bitter, and I was ashamed to find myself thinking, Thank God, it's he that's getting hurt and not I. But though the occasion was hideously uncomfortable, I was grateful to my employer for having kept me up to the mark.

Unfortunately, I was not grateful enough. My second summer at Martha's Vineyard I met the poet and radical writer Max Eastman, a former editor of *The Masses* who, with the other editors, had twice been on trial after World War I under the Sedition Act of 1917 because *The Masses* had opposed America's participation in the war. Unlike most radical intellectuals, Eastman was as beautiful as an army with banners. Though a big man, he had a lithe, catlike walk and long before bright-colored clothes for men were an accepted thing, he wore cherry-red or pale blue slacks that made him seem, among the conventionally clad males, like some kind of messenger from Olympus.

Max Eastman persuaded me—without, I am sorry to say, too much difficulty—that the welfare of the oppressed classes required that I should work for him rather than for a paternalistic entrepreneur like Tom Stix, and as he would brook no delay, I left Mr. Stix without giving him anything like proper notice. My rationalizations for this self-indulgent step could not have been described as anything but shabby.

I was dazzled by Max Eastman's looks, by the charm and playful wit he could exert when he chose, by his poetry and by his prose style, which had a kind of classical rhythm to it, like the swags on an Adam mantel. In his radicalism, however, I took little interest. Eastman spoke Russian and had married a Russian wife, and at that time—when most intellectuals were disposed to admire the Soviets and turn a blind eye to their faults—he was writing a book called *Artists in Uniform*. This book was an angry and eloquent protest against the Soviet dictum that writers must put their talents at the service of the state. Eastman wrote with passion and fervor, but I typed out the whole manuscript of *Artists in Uniform* without learning much more than that there was a fellow named Trotsky who had been done wrong to.

Max had, however, written an excellent book called *Enjoyment of Poetry* and this I read through twice, not missing a word. I wrote some poetry of my own and Max praised it, though I had a faint suspicion, from something in the tone of his voice, that the praise may have been in part compensatory, deriving from the fact that he was not able to pay me very much. He did however tell me that I ought to become a writer, and when I said I did not want to, he said that was because I was lazy and selfish.

Despite this stricture, which I shrugged off, I felt intensely and romantically loyal to him and defended him staunchly against his critcs. He had plenty of them, and the ones who talked to me were not outraged by his radicalism, but offended because Max did not have a mere two legs on the Self-Absorption Trophy. He had already won it. Hands down. Eastman had known what it was, during the anti-Bolshevist frenzy after World War I, to have citizens with guns lurking in the bushes outside his house waiting to take potshots at him. But, astonishing in a professional revolutionary, he was like a cat in his love of comfort—of good food, soft beds, pretty young women and expensive cigars.

He was a hard worker, and did not spare himself the long hours at the desk, but as he grew older the love of comfort seemed to take him over. Ten years after my stint with him, he accepted a job as roving editor of *The Reader's Digest*, which was an odd assignment for what had once been an unsparingly analytical intellect. Ten years after that, the former editor of *The Masses*, that great landmark in the history of the American left, was making speeches in support of Senator Joseph McCarthy.

I worked for Eastman for the better part of a year and then, when he had to go on an extended lecture trip, he got me a job with his publishers, Simon and Schuster—a bit of gainful employment which led to my getting married and starting to write. In that order.

Simon and Schuster had been launched a decade before by Richard Simon and Max Schuster and had put itself on the map, in its first year of business, by having a great success with the first crossword puzzle books. In 1937, it was to coin money with Dale Carnegie's *How to Win Friends and Influence People*. Even before that, the long-established publishing houses looked down their noses at S. and S. as being brash and *arriviste*, but the firm could undoubtedly sell books, so it was not without distinguished authors on its list.

I went to work as secretary to Mr. Simon. Six feet four inches tall, with a long-lashed and blue-eyed gaze that would have set the Statue of Liberty panting, Dick Simon had been

a favored child of fortune all his life. He was such a gifted
pianist that it had been touch and go whether he would start
a publishing firm or go on the concert stage, and when he
took up photography he was so brilliant at it that top-flight
professionals treated him with respect. Rather conspicuously
weak, sometimes, on orderly thought processes, he was nevertheless capable of great leaps of the imagination which left
more disciplined intellects standing at the post.

In mellow mood, Dick Simon was the world's most
charming companion to high and low alike, and when he
made up his mind to be persuasive, he could turn solid
granite into aluminum foil. But he was arbitrary, capricious
and unpredictable, bestowing favors here and snatching them
away there in a fashion which reduced people to helpless
rage. Nevertheless, S. and S. was famous for the effectiveness
of its promotion and the pulling power of its ads, and this was
because Mr. Simon could not tolerate boredom and would
only employ persons who had originality and could amuse
him.

One such employee was Clifton Fadiman, who was
head of the Editorial Department and for whom I sometimes
worked when Mr. Simon was out of town. Fadiman was at
that time moonlighting as book critic of *The New Yorker*,
though his famous radio program, *Information, Please*, still
lay ahead. At S. and S. he was the Office Iconoclast. In
order to bait Mr. Simon, who had a puritanical streak, he
used what were in those days blunt and shocking words, like
"masturbation," and the first morning I walked into his office, he glared at me and said, "Say 'balls,' Miss Halsey."

I felt as if I had been hit across the back of the knees
with a telephone pole, but I managed to rally.

"Plain, or with an accent?" I said.

But we got on well together, in the event, and he once

said to me approvingly, "You have an unerring eye for a phony."

The people who worked for S. and S. had an unusual *esprit de corps*. They were all young, bright and ambitious and I was a kind of mascot—the snowy little goat that runs out on the football field ahead of the team—because, alone among them, I was totally without ambition and therefore no threat to anybody. With great trepidation I had moved out of my parents' house and gone to live in New York, but that change of venue seemed to have exhausted my initiative.

Basically, what I wanted out of life was to sit in an oriel window somewhere and read the classics of literature, while in the background a shadowy husband figure paid the bills and appreciated me. Consciously or unconsciously, my fellow workers realized what I myself had not the slightest inkling of—namely, that the key to my character was dependence. They decided, like a covey of Jewish mothers, to get me married and the person they hit upon as a suitable match was Henry Simon, Dick Simon's next youngest brother.

They found both Henry and me willing to fall in with their plan, though we were neither of us head-over-heels in love. We liked each other's looks; Henry, who was some years older than I, thought it was about time for him to get married; and I wanted someone to take care of me. Looking back on it, I think the romance for both of us lay in getting married at all, for marriage in those days was still considered a binding, long-term commitment and a sacrament and still had the faint fairy-tale promise of living happily ever after.

The Simons were a prosperous and tightly knit German-Jewish family and Henry was a gentle soul—slight of build but tall, and with a poet's profile—who had all his life had to live in the shadow of the meteoric Dick. But he had his own distinction. He was a professor of English at Teachers College, Columbia, and years later I would sometimes run across people who had been students of Henry's and whose faces would light up at the mention of his name.

Early in our acquaintance I said to him that I did not think of him as Jewish. An expression I could not read went across his face. "That's a very anti-Semitic remark," he said quietly. I was speechless, having seen in one unnerving flash the truth of what he said.

Henry and I were married very quietly, and one way or another anti-Semitism seemed to have a good deal to do with our nuptials. After we had decided to get married, I called up my mother in a state of great exhilaration to tell her the news. There was a long silence on the telephone. Then she said, "Well! You know what I think about the Jews!" and hung up. The next day she telephoned to say that she had been thinking it over—there was some indication that Reinhold had had a hand in the thinking—and that perhaps after all she should not have said such a thing. Suffused with embarrassment, I stammered, "Oh, that's all right," and changed the subject.

In marrying Henry I discovered something that, as a sheltered South Yonkers WASP, I had had no suspicion of—which was that in those days very few New York apartment buildings would rent to Jews. About Annie's anti-Semitic remark I had not been conscious of having any feelings at all, but at this example of prejudice and bigotry, I was outraged. I could think of nothing practical to do about the situation, but I hated to have to take it lying down and somewhere within me there arose an inchoate premonition that I was not going to be able to be "flexible" and to accept without protest, as the way of the world, unfairness and injustice.

The relationship between Henry and me was unbelievably tranquil and unmarred by quarrels. This was partly because I was so fervently grateful to him for taking me out of

the world of business. Even more, it was because I was getting my own way and had nothing about which to be dissatisfied or resentful. I hated domesticity, so—although we could
not really afford it—we had a young girl who came in every
day to clean the apartment and cook the dinner, while I went
to Columbia University to get my Master's. Principally,
however, our domestic serenity was owing to the fact that
Henry and I, almost from the moment of our meeting, had
slipped into a teacher-pupil relationship.

Extremely conscious of the lacunae in my education, I
was a willing student of anything. The Simons all spoke German, so Henry and I began going through a first-year German grammar. The Simons were steeped to the eyebrows in
music, so I read music appreciation books, and when Henry
and I went to concerts, I took the scores with me, with
themes, bridging passages and cadenzas all marked out.
Henry did not himself have the inflexible Teutonic methodi-
calness which I had inherited from Reinhold, but he had
seen it before. It was not new to him.

The second year of our marriage I at last started to write.
Henry got an exchange professorship with a man at the University of the Southwest, which was a branch of London University located at Exeter, in Devon. Foreign travel was less
commonplace in those days than it is now, but Henry had
studied at Oxford and been to Europe on several other occasions, so he was calm about it. I was not. My childhood
had been spent soaking up Dickens and Thackeray, but what
one acquired from a Lincoln Park upbringing was Small Expectations. I had never thought to set foot in the Mother
Country at all, much less take up residence there for a year.

Potsdam, New York—where I had once gone to visit a
friend and taken the sleeper home—had up till then been my
idea of Ultima Thule; and as we stood on the deck of the
Cunarder and watched the pier receding, I felt that compared

to me, Marco Polo had been a paraplegic. I was incandescent, and Henry put an arm around me and said laughingly, "When you look like that, I'm putty in your hands."

Arrived in the United Kingdom, we rented a house in an idyllic little village near Exeter, and with the house came a maid so perfectly trained as to be a kind of female Jeeves. In those days, just before World War II, the English were still riddled with class consciousness, and I quickly discovered that if I performed any action at all around the house—aside from "doing the flahrs" after breakfast in the morning—our maid would lose caste with other people's maids. Henry was in Exeter all day, and since I was thrust into the role of aristocratic idleness, I had a lot of time on my hands and I spent much of it writing letters to my friends at home.

There was a good deal to write about. The English at that time, still masters of an Empire, were unbelievably condescending to Americans. Patronage and conscious superiority to the crude colonials from across the water exuded from their pores; and my national identity being thus devalued, I discovered that I had a measure of pride in it. America meant Franklin and Eleanor Roosevelt, and beating back the Depression, and that famous, spellbinding voice on the radio saying, "We have nothing to fear but fear itself." I was fascinated by the survivals from English history—the thousand-year-old cathedrals, the Black Prince's armor, the quaint formalities of Parliament—but felt that Abraham Lincoln could hold his own with all of them.

Therefore, though supremely happy to be living in England, I was not so reverently Anglophile that I forgot to keep score. The rose-embowered cottages that, along with the fourteenth-century church, made our village so picturesque were dark and damp and smelly inside, and those thatched roofs sometimes harbored vermin. And while my friend and hero, Charles Dickens, had written a great deal about his countrymen's rosy cheeks, he had never said a word about their teeth, and this was obviously because he had seen so few of them. The English smile was a two-inch-wide casualty list, and this was true whether the smile belonged to the rural working class who lived in the thatched cottages or the gentlefolk who, in our village, kept a pack and rode to hounds with all the panoply of "pink" coats, stirrup cups and the occasional fatal spill.

These and other meditations and reflections I put into my letters to the States, and before long I myself got a communication from Dick Simon. He sent me all the letters he had been able to collect that I had written to my friends at S. and S., and he told me that I was to use them as a model and write a book. The note of command, the expectation of being obeyed, were unmistakable. The working title of the book, he said, would be *Travel Diary of a Professor's Wife*—we would think of a better one later—and he enclosed a check for $250 as an advance.

I complied immediately. As my former boss and the head of my husband's family, Mr. Simon was an authority figure, and if there was one thing I had been used to right from the cradle, it was having orders barked at me. My intuitive brother-in-law had realized what others had not—which was that to get me started writing, it was not necessary to flatter and encourage. All you had to do was say, "*Achtung!*"

Our year in England came to an end. We returned to the States, and I finished the book in the winter of 1937–38. The actual job of writing, of committing myself irretrievably to paper, quickly demonstrated that the decorous behavior on which I prided myself was only a veneer. Underneath was the usual writer's temperament—the violent sensitivity to criticism, the moods of despair that brooked no word of comfort and the imperious, the almost disgusting, need for praise. Henry was patient and unfailingly supportive, though he

must sometimes have felt—confronted with all this intensity
and unreasonableness—like one who is trying to hold down
the Graf Zeppelin with a length of basting thread. In the
end, however, when despite all clutchings at the forehead the
job was finally done, Dick Simon was delighted with it. He
said, moreover, that the book was going to sell.

In this opinion he was alone. With one of those gau-
cheries of which he was sometimes capable, he sent me the
reports which had been written on the manuscript by my
former colleagues at S. and S. These people had had no idea
I would ever read what they said and, while they conceded
the stuff was not unfunny, saw no market for it because making fun of the English was old hat and had already been done
to death.

"Oh, boy, are they wrong!" said Mr. Simon in his cov-
ering note.

It was Dick Simon who came up with the title—*With
Malice Toward Some*. Publication was set for August, and
Henry and I went to Vermont for the summer. Nothing
could shake Dick Simon's ebullient confidence in the book's
sales potential, but Henry and I, to protect ourselves from
disappointment, latched onto the manuscript readers' view.
My principal worry—which I did not dare tell anyone because it was so egocentric—was that war would break out in
Europe and my poor little book would be sunk without a
trace in the great crashing breakers of History.

We all knew that war was coming. Those Americans
who cared about the fate of freely elected, constitutional governments had watched with anguish while the Spanish Loy-
alists went down to defeat, and I had, while we were in
Devonshire, gone to Germany for a week without Henry to
get some money out for a refugee girl in Exeter.

The people with whom I stayed in Germany had a yel-
low sign on their front gate saying, "Beware! Jews live here,"

and every time you raised your eyes from the ground, somebody gave the Nazi salute and said, "Heil Hitler!" The death camps were not to be set up for another five years, but the atmosphere of cultism was like a strangling, suffocating sewer gas. I worshiped Franklin Roosevelt as only I could worship, but I could not imagine myself or any other American flapping an arm, like a penguin which had just taken a charge of buckshot in the chest, and saying, "Heil Roosevelt!"

War was in the air, in that summer of 1938, but Henry and I, in Vermont, were soon to be distracted from the ominous rumblings in Europe. We had rented a little house high up on the side of a mountain and it had no telephone. We had been there only a few days when I got a message to go down the hill and call New York. I did, and was told that the Book-of-the-Month Club had chosen *With Malice* as a dual selection. Book clubs were a new thing in those days, and a book club choice had much more impact than it was to have later, when such clubs had proliferated all over the place.

The book club selection was entirely owing to Dick Simon. The book had been rated "C" by its first reader at the Book-of-the-Month Club, and only books rated "A" were sent to the judges. When Mr. Simon heard this, he called the president of the Book-of-the-Month Club and asked him to read *With Malice* himself. Yielding to the Simon persuasiveness, the president did, and marked it "A."

I heard the news and ran panting up the mountainside to tell Henry. When we had finished dancing around, he asked me how much money I would get.

"I don't know," I said, "but it had the word 'thousand' in it."

The book came out in mid-August and succeeded beyond anyone's wildest dreams, even Dick Simon's. It was reviewed everywhere, even in *Women's Wear Daily*, and the reviewers threw their caps in the air with loud hurrahs. Actually, the reviews consisted mostly of quotes from the book, but there was no mistaking the fact that *With Malice* had struck a chord. It will seem incredible to young people today, but there was a time when Americans had a streak of meekness and acquiescence in their nature. For a hundred years before *With Malice* came out, Englishmen had been making tidy sums of money by coming over here and telling American lecture audiences that they were crude and uncivilized. The judgment was accepted without dispute, but underneath it was resented, and a review of *With Malice* in one of the New York Sunday papers expressed a general feeling with the heading, THE ENGLISH: THEY HAD IT COMING TO THEM.

I must have been asked hundreds of times, both then and later, how it felt to find myself all of a sudden the author of a runaway best seller.

It felt exquisite.

The ego massage was voluptuous beyond description.

When I was thirteen years old and crazy about the movies, I used sometimes to buy a movie magazine and an Oh Henry bar and take them up to the attic for a secret session of luxurious enjoyment. The success of *With Malice* reminded me of those Oh Henry bars. Juices of surpassing sweetness flowed over the tongue.

I was—to change the metaphor—the bride in a wedding that went on and on. S. and S. subscribed to a clipping service for me, and fistfuls of clippings arrived in every mail. Fan letters started pouring in which brimmed with praise. It was a narcissist's paradise, and the atmosphere of excitement and exhilaration never flagged. The sales figures were telephoned up from New York once and sometimes twice a day, while quiet-spoken Henry was so proud of me he almost purred. Dick had always been the meteor in the Simon fam-

ily, but now the next youngest brother—hitherto thrown into
the shade by Richard's brilliance—had a meteor of his own.

Actually, this saturnalia of felicity was a little more than
one could take in. A friend of mine once said that new evening clothes do not really belong to you until you have been
hot in them. I suddenly found myself wearing the most beautiful evening dress in the world, but I had not been hot in it.
I had not written several books and gradually built up an audience. I had served no punitive apprenticeship to achieve
this success. I was shining-eyed and incredibly thrilled and
happy; and if Henry and I did not actually drink champagne
for breakfast, lunch and dinner, that was pretty much the
way it seemed. Once in a while, however—for all the nectar
and ambrosia of being deferred to and of being the un-
displaceable center of attention—once in a while I felt wood-
eny, as if, like a mannequin in a store window, I had no
sweat glands.

And there was a gnawing little anxiety which I kept to
myself. I knew that this Mardi Gras could not last. Over and
over, I reminded myself of that. The day would finally come
when *With Malice* was no longer at the top of the best-seller
list. And how would I feel then? Would I be eaten up with
jealousy when some other book succeeded mine in everybody's conversation? Having once been, temporarily, so important, would I be able to reconcile myself to being unimportant again?

It did not occur to me that the unimportance would be
relative. Even when *With Malice* was last year's phenomenon, it would still be a long time before I was a complete and
total nobody. Henry could have told me this. I might have
known it myself, since I had worked for a publisher. But my
mind saw everything in terms of black and white, so I was denied the comfort of realizing that the excitement would in all

probability taper off slowly enough for me to accommodate to
its decline—the more so as American life did not move as
fast in 1938 as it does now.

But the sic-transit-gloria angle was far from being
enough of a haunt to spoil things. The money, I was told,
was pouring in like water from a faucet. Henry and I both
had modest tastes and a predilection for the quiet, academic
life, so extravagant uses of the money did not spring to either
of our minds. You could, without arousing a storm of protest, have described us as rather a dull couple. At any rate, it
was taken for granted that the money would be invested in
insurance and annuities. The money, actually, did not stand
out by itself. It was part of the shimmering haze in which everything was enveloped. But sometimes awareness of the
money would suddenly sweep over me—a sense of the mag-
nificent enhancement of self it brought with it—and I would
feel a stab of pure ecstasy.

These were the intoxicating gratifications. There were
soberer pleasures, too. Mrs. Kelly wrote me a letter in which
the curlicues of her beautiful penmanship were matched by
curlicues of sentimentality about myself as a child in the
sixth grade. She wished that Miss Sibley could have been
alive—a wish that echoed poignantly in my own heart. The
Boltons, fortunately, were still very much in their prime.
When I went to work in the bank, I had given Dr. Bolton's
name as a reference and he had responded with a letter saying that I was the best writer who had ever gone through
Skidmore. Felix had the letter on his desk when I went for
my interview, and tapping it with his solid-gold Eversharp
pencil, he had said grimly, "There'll be no need for that
here." (Actually, there was, since Mr. Raven's own prose
reminded one of Civil War artillery horses struggling to get a
cannon out of the mud, and I fixed it up.) I think it was a
source of particular satisfaction to Dr. Bolton that his judg-

ment had been vindicated in the only terms that Felix would have understood—namely, financial success.

Among the soberer pleasures of success was the fact that, because of *With Malice*, I met and got to know Dorothy Canfield Fisher, who lived the year round on the same mountain in Arlington, Vermont, where Henry and I were spending the summer. Mrs. Fisher's novels are no longer known to a general public, but at that time she had such a devoted readership that tourists often made their way to her remote little house and hovered about, hoping for a glimpse of her. She was unique. A graduate of the Sorbonne, a musician and an accomplished linguist, she was at the same time homespun in the best sense of that word. To me and to many others she represented the New England conscience at its finest, and I was to remain a friend of hers for the rest of her life. At the time, I felt that Providence had brought me to her particular mountainside so that the renown she had—and had had for a long time—would be a lesson to me not to get too much puffed up with my little one-shot performance.

But while these intangible pleasures were being vouchsafed, sales of the book were vaulting and the publishers asked me if I did not want to come down to New York and enjoy bestsellerdom in person. However, I preferred to stay in Vermont. There was no need for me to push the book personally, and I was not by nature or training a crowd-pleaser—a characteristic about which I was revoltingly complacent.

Today the writer not only has to write his book. He is also supposed to sell it by going on television, signing autographs, being interviewed for magazines, appearing at literary luncheons and in general proclaiming to an inattentive world, "Look at me, fellas, I'm dancin'!" This obligatory and exhausting routine is known to the trade as "the bicycle ride." In 1938, however, the bicycle ride existed only in embryonic form and you could sidestep it without being considered a self-willed eccentric.

In actual fact, I had work to do which I knew I could not get done in the midst of a throng of people. The book had been sold to an English publisher and a tedious and fussy revision job was called for because of the English libel laws, which are much more fanged than those of the United States. But the summer waned. Henry's school opened and he went back to the city. I stayed on for a while, but finally it was necessary for me to pack my bags and return to the wider world and the bitch goddess in her modest, pre-World War II incarnation.

4

I Snuff the Air,
I Paw the Tainted Ground

The first thing I had to do when I got back to New York was to go and see my family. I found them somewhat altered. While Henry and I were in England, Reinhold had retired and bought a house in Newtown, Connecticut. The house was carpenter Gothic, but commodious, and Annie—feeling that she now had a suitable background—had abandoned the role of recluse and embarked on a modest social life.

But what had been advantageous for her had been, initially, a disaster for my father. In the olden days, before we all got so fluent and insightful about human behavior, hideous things could go on in families without a word being spoken about them. My mother did not tell me until years later, but after he retired, my father had a severe nervous breakdown. It was apparently the usual crisis of the hardworking man coming unprepared to leisure, exacerbated in Reinhold's case by the undiluted society of Annie. Exacerbated also, no doubt, by the passion and energy of his nature.

My mother, telling me about it a long time afterward, said in her unaccented way that she had been afraid he would kill himself. If even the unresponsive Annie felt apprehension, things must have been bad. Nowadays we say to

people going through emotional crises, "You must get help."
But Reinhold had no help at all. No tranquilizers, no psychiatrist and no deep religious belief. And because of Annie's
ban on visitors during her long recluse period, he had no
friends of many years' standing to whom he could unburden
himself.

I do not like to think of what, completely alone, my father must have gone through. But somehow,

> Out of the night that covered him,
> Black as the pit from pole to pole,

he apparently worked out some kind of salvation. Did he find
some philosopher or diarist whose books provided occasional
support? Did some childhood memory hold him back from
the uttermost brink of despair? I did not know, when I saw
him again, what he had been through, but I did perceive that
he was changed. There was now a note of acceptance and
resignation in his attitude toward his wife.

Contemplating at this distance in time my father's long-
forgotten "shipwreck of the soul," as John Clare has called it,
I am reminded of the old Norse proverb that says, "Heroism
consists of hanging on one minute longer." And it may have
been that the success of *With Malice* added, for Reinhold,
one tiny grace note to his obscure but monumental self-res-
cue, for he shook me warmly by the hand and said, "A fine
job, Margaret, a very fine job," and it was clear that he was
enormously proud of me.

My sister proffered conventional congratulations on my
good fortune, but to her it must have been a reenactment in
spades of my getting skipped in P.S. 21. She had married a
man who was some kind of builder or building contractor.
He had an engineering degree, but my mother thought he
was not good enough to have married into our family. In this

she was quite wrong. My father had started his career in a factory and my mother's father had worked in a factory all his life, so the giddy social eminence we occupied was not much higher than the callus on a workingman's palm.

As a child, Mary's most outstanding characteristic had seemed to me to be laziness and a notable capacity for sliding out of household tasks. Whenever there were dishes to be done, she went to the bathroom, and was deaf to all the poundings on the door. As a last resort, I washed exactly half the dishes—a mathematical calculation of great delicacy which was the only kind of arithmetic I was any good at—but my unsympathetic parents, blind to the staring claims of justice, only said impatiently, "What's the matter? Are you afraid of work?"

In my sister's case, however, the child was not father to the man, for as a married woman she was a whirlwind of energy. She taught school and kept house and did besides a great many strenuous things like wallpapering and dressmaking. I do not believe that either she or my mother ever finished reading With Malice. It was very far from being their cup of tea. But they had their own kind of dignity, and they did not try in any way to use me or to exploit my temporary prominence.

However, if my relatives had no wish to move in on me, the society itself apparently did. It is all laid out for you, when you suddenly have a popular best seller. Or at least it was in those days. You were to sell the book to the movies. You were to go out to Hollywood yourself and write for the movies. You were to move into the luxury apartment—not because, in your heart, you were ready for it, but because the failure to do so would be construed as a reproach. And before you knew what had happened, you were the captive of a standard of living.

But through sheer dumb instinct I managed to stay out of the trap. I had the Sealed Mind of the Halseys and Small Expectations, and it takes more than Western capitalism to make a dent in *that*. However, there still remained the problem of what to do with the freedom I had managed to preserve. To that question, I was a long time in finding an answer.

In the meantime, I lived in an atmosphere of blandishments. After I had been back from Vermont for some weeks, Dick Simon did a thing which at that time had never been done in publishing, though it has become a commonplace since. On the theory that nothing succeeds like success, he took the whole back page of *The Times* on several occasions to advertise the book. This was long before the days when people bought full-page ads in *The Times* on behalf of good causes, and the sheer unaccustomed acreage of Mr. Simon's advertisements—let alone what the ads actually said—made my head swim.

Other, more modest little goodies rolled out of Destiny's cornucopia, each producing its inward surge of half-incredulous delight. Several times, riding in the subway, I saw someone in the same car reading *With Malice* and laughing. Walking along the street, I would see the book lying on the seats of parked cars. When I stopped in at Simon and Schuster, where only two years before I had been taking dictation, heads popped out of doors and smiles raced like brushfire along the corridors. Nobody actually asked me to touch them for the King's Evil, but that was the general climate.

Nevertheless, Henry and I did not change our way of life. We spent the evenings at home reading aloud or—since Henry played the viola—sometimes having people in for string quartets. I quickly gave up going to parties, for I soon discovered that I could not carry off either mindless adulation which was out of all proportion to the circumstances or, on the other hand, remarks in which envy was not very well concealed. But though I stayed away from large gatherings, the *tête-à-tête* was something else again, and I was taken to lunch every day by friends, well-wishers, editors, agents and all kinds of literary folk.

These lunches were always at restaurants where the menus had tassels on them and the martinis were so big that you could easily mistake the olive at the bottom for a mermaid. In those pre-television days, celebrities did not come and go so fast as they do now, and occasionally I was aware that I was being unobtrusively pointed out to people. I schooled the face to composure, but inside my rib cage a nest of singing birds started caroling as if it were dawn on a May morning.

Those lunches were as glamorous as the most schoolgirlish heart could wish, but underneath the glamour a tussle was going on that had its comic aspects. Everyone wanted me to write another book as soon as possible. It was suggested repeatedly that I should buy a ticket to another country and do *With Malice* all over again, using a different set of foreigners. These urgings did not spring from crude self-interest, since the people who took me to lunch often did not stand to gain anything by my reaping a second harvest from a second book. Nor was the pressure crudely expressed, since my companions were urbane and civilized people. But an admonition can sometimes come through just as strongly from the urbane and civilized as through the clamor of Birchites and hardhats.

Nobody was importunate—at least, most people were not—but I nevertheless had the sense of being crowded. One was not expected to be openly greedy—that, in fact, would be deplorable—but one did not let the chance slip to cash in to the last penny on Fortune's favor. It wouldn't be normal.

I wish I could say that I resisted these nudgings with such eloquence that prisoners of success and standard-of-living captives all over the country bedewed my garments with grateful tears. But what made the situation comic was that I was unaware of a rather stringent limitation in my character—which was, that the Girl in the Glacier was unable to confide. I had modeled myself with too slavish a devotion on a lady who was fond of saying, "I pride myself on my reserve." In conversation I could be lively enough, particularly with the help of a drink or two, but my real feelings never found their way into words—though a far-from-poker face would have kept anyone from describing me as enigmatic.

This emotional lockjaw prevented me from telling anyone—even Henry—that I was bored to death with *With Malice*. It had been a good little vein while it lasted, but the vein was worked out. Were I to do another book, I wanted it to be in some way different. But different in what direction? I knew that I was a small-bore writer and not a Gun of Navarone, but what could I do within the limits of small-borishness that would be something of a departure from what I had just finished doing?

I had not the faintest idea.

Nevertheless, through the softly swirling fog in my head a bell buoy kept sounding, tolling out a warning that if I were too obliging and submissive, I would end up as a hack humorist, grinding out exaggerated similes and metaphors because they were expected of me and brought in the shekels, but with spontaneity slowly withering in my harnessed soul.

They were very gay, those lunches, with both parties having a sportive romp through the old vocabulary, with much svelte self-mockery (not really believed) and with glasses raised to toast the success of the book. Underneath, however, I was defending my lightheartedness with all the

solemnity of an earnest puritan nature. And my luckless part-
ners, on their side, were like people tapping on a wall to
locate the beam and never managing to evoke the proper
clunky sound.

Dick Simon, however, found the beam right away. He
took me to lunch at "21," where I had not been before and
which I did not find reassuring. The tables were too small
and too close together. I liked to eat at tables like prairies
which were spaced so that adjacent diners could not over-
hear. These tables, however, did not need to be either large
or private, since they were less for eating than for hopping.
The clientele was going to and fro as if they were on the
Stock Exchange.

Dick, however, immediately gave me a sense of security. This was something he could do for people when he
chose to—he became a sort of combination of *grand seigneur*
and wise old family doctor—and at the moment, he very
much chose to. He was proud of himself for having spotted a
best seller that nobody else had seen and proud of me because, as Henry's wife, I had brought distinction to the
Simon clan.

"I've just come from an editorial meeting," he said, as
soon as we had given our order, "and everybody wants to
know about your next book."

My heart sank, but he went on to say just the opposite of
what I expected to hear.

"Ignore them. Don't listen to anything but your own
mind. Wait until you're really ready to do another book,
even if it seems forever."

I was speechless with gratitude. Here was Authority, and
it spoke in perfect accordance with my own wishes—which,
in my past experience, Authority had not been very prone to
do.

"The next book can wait," he went on, "but there's

something that has to be dealt with right away, and that is the offers coming in from Hollywood."

I was twenty-eight years old, but a girl of twelve could have shown me cards and spades when it came to knowledge of the world. It was not that I had lacked the opportunity to learn, but that it did not attract me as a field of study.

"I've heard of them," I said. "Or at least Henry has."

"I asked you to lunch," Dick said, "for the special purpose of begging you not to go out to the Coast and write for the movies."

"I wouldn't dream of it! Henry wouldn't be able to go with me. I'd have to go alone. . . ." I let my voice trail off, contemplating a prospect that, for me, had all the allure of a tankful of piranhas.

Dick reached across the table and covered my hand with his own, which was warm and firm.

At that moment there was a slight distraction. Two very red-faced priests were being seated at a table near us with many attendant flourishes. We both looked at them and I said, "Mendicants, I presume."

Dick laughed. "Underneath that apparent shyness," he said, "you're a crusty provincial.

"But," he continued, "there are some people out there who want to buy the book and make a film out of it."

"I don't want to sell it."

Dick looked at me in astonishment.

"You told me," I said defensively, "not to listen to anything but my own mind."

"Touché," he replied, with a disarming grin.

"There's no possible way to make a movie out of With Malice. It has some funny cracks, but as Henry says, the characters are strictly one-dimensional. And there's no plot. No story line whatsoever."

"They fix that up," Dick replied good-naturedly.

"That's just it. They'll sling together some kind of Boy-Meets-Girl mishmash that will resemble *With Malice* about as much as *With Malice* resembles *Jane's Fighting Ships*." I had come a long way since my high school infatuation with the output of Hollywood.

"But what do you care? You'll make a lot of money out of it. And so, incidentally, will your publishers."

"It's *my* book. It's got my name on it. In a way, I'm responsible for it."

I hesitated.

"I feel possessive about it. I don't want it bracketed with a hunk of trash."

"A contract could be written that would give you control over the making of the movie."

I looked at him and we both laughed. I had told Henry, and Henry had told Dick, about a chance meeting I had had, on one of the many occasions when I was being taken to lunch, with a celebrated movie tycoon. I do not now remember his name, save that it was always uttered with bated breath. This potentate had put his navel on the table, about four inches in from the edge, and talked from there, meanwhile waving in my face a cigar that was as much saliva as tobacco and referring to *With Malice* as "the proppity." For the part of Henry in the film, he said, he wanted "somebody dinnified like Clock Gable."

My chances of controlling that kind of patron of the arts seemed minimal.

"I have no dependents," I said. "There's nobody, old or young, who's going to reproach me with not having provided for them."

"I'm not trying to pressure you."

These are words which very seldom have the ring of truth, but this time they did.

"I'm being the devil's advocate. You and Henry might

have children. You don't have to spend the money now. You can tuck it away somewhere. Nobody knows what the future holds."

A man passing by stopped and greeted Dick effusively. He seemed prepared to launch a conversation, but Mr. Simon was abrupt and dismissive.

"Trading on the title," I said, "to sell something that would *have* to be completely unrelated to the original book—and something that would in all probability be cheap and visibly exploitative—seems to me to be a fraud on the public."

"It wouldn't really be a fraud, because the public is used to that sort of thing. They've come to expect it."

Although my publisher was making a case, he was not being disputatious about it. His manner was relaxed and cheerful, so I was able to stick to my guns without panicking and growing quaveringly obstinate.

"A confidence trick that is sanctioned by custom is still a confidence trick."

I frowned.

"Whatever it might be for others, it's just not right for me. It doesn't feel right."

He nodded. He, who himself operated so largely on intuition, could understand its importance to others. But then his face sobered.

"Now I have to tell you something."

There was a slight but pregnant pause.

"The contract you signed with Simon and Schuster gives us the right to sell the book, whether or not you approve."

I was completely taken aback. I had signed the contract without reading it, though Henry had read it, but at that time all Henry and I hoped for was that the book would sell enough copies so that I would not have to scrub floors in my publisher's office to pay back the advance.

"But if you don't want to sell it, we won't sell it. I don't share your feelings, but I respect them."

"Oh!" I breathed. My vision was not so narrow and blinkered that I failed to appreciate the princeliness of the gesture. "If this weren't such a public place, I'd lean across this table and kiss you."

My eye was caught by a ripple of flame and I saw that the two priests were about to be served with crêpes suzette. I nodded in their direction.

"They're impostors," I said. "You're the one who should have your collar on backwards."

He laughed. "I'm *parsona grata*," he said.

Though I had not mentioned it to Mr. Simon, the question raised in my mind by the issue of selling *With Malice* to the movies was: What was the hurry? If I were going to sell a book to the movies, why not wait until I had written a book the movies could genuinely use? I was not so old that this was my last chance to earn money. It was the matter of selling my first book to the movies that put into my mind something which has influenced my thinking ever since— namely, that there is a good deal of illogic and unreason in much that is generally accepted without question as sensible and rational.

I had been all compact of high principles about *With Malice* and Hollywood, but high principles, unhappily, can all too easily decelerate into priggishness, and I went very fast from the sublime to the meticulous. The fan mail kept coming in, and I answered all the letters myself. One day a lady editor said impatiently that I ought to hire a secretary to do all that and get on with writing another book. With a really repellant piety I answered that if people took the trouble to write to me, I felt I owed it to them to reply personally. I was not so besotted with conscious virtue as to miss the look that flashed across her face, and made a mental note never to say *that* again.

The fact was that the lady editor had caught me out in a piece of plain fakery. Many of the letters were inconsequential or even downright silly, and the reason I answered them all was not that I had a sensitive finger on the pulse of humanity, but simply that I could not think of anything else to do with my time. I could not write. Too many eyes were upon me and I was paralyzed with self-consciousness. And outside of writing, there were no prospects that beckoned. I was qualified to teach, but had no vocation for it and was relieved that I would not have to do it. The one excuse that everyone would have accepted for my not writing would have been if I had started a family. But I was terrified of being pregnant—of walking about with a two-foot projection in front of my spine which would proclaim to everyone that I was no longer *virgo intacta*. This, too, however, was one of the things I could not articulate.

In the dim and distant days before Freud, we all believed that when you reached the age of twenty-one, your character was formed. If you had been lucky enough to have proper, respectable parents, they would have formed it into a good one and from then on, you could forget about it. It was there and it was reliable and it would see you through all vicissitudes. My parents might have been a little arbitrary, but they were obviously the best character developers since the invention of the cold shower and the hair shirt. It therefore did not cross my mind that I could be unsettled in any major way by the unexpected success of *With Malice*. But as Dick Simon had said in another connection, "Oh, boy, was I wrong!"

Just a year after the book had come out, I started going
to a psychiatrist. Psychoanalysis was a new thing in those
days and the New York intellectuals had embraced it with
fervor. Henry and several of his friends had a pet healer
named Dr. S., to whom they had all been at one time or
another, and almost from Henry's and my first meeting, he
had urged me to be analyzed. He was so keen on it that, even
before we thought of being married, he was going to pay for
it. But I used to laugh and say, "I don't need analysis. I had a
happy childhood."

Nothing is less riveting than the tribulations of the Poor
Little Rich Girl, so it will suffice to say that success had left
me directionless and what we would now call unmotivated.

"If I am a one-book writer," I said to Henry, "I want to
be the kind of one-book writer who writes only one book."

But had I truly shot my bolt? Confused and unable to
think for myself, I nevertheless did not warm to the thinking
which other people, at my request, did for me. So after a
year during which the poor, the ill and the luckless would
have considered themselves thrice blessed to have problems
like mine, I at last bent the knee to fashion and started seeing
Dr. S.

Though some people swore by Dr. S., there were others
who thought less highly of him, and ignorant armies clashing
by night would have been a fair description of the relationship between him and me, for we were both armed and
we were certainly both ignorant. Psychoanalysis in those days
had not yet benefited from the insights of such writers as
Karen Horney, Harry Stack Sullivan, Erich Fromm, Rollo
May, Erik Erikson and others. It was thus in an undeveloped
stage at best, but as practiced by Dr. S., it was not only undeveloped, it was primitive.

Not that there was anything primitive about the doctor's
establishment. His office was at a fashionable address and the

waiting room, large and softly lit, was furnished with chintz-covered chairs and sofa, expensive reproductions of Colonial furniture and suitable prints on the walls. The secretary wore a nurse's uniform and tiptoed, and the doctor himself affected a white coat. The atmosphere was a judicious blend of medicalness and comfort, and the premises had a special exit in the rear so that the patients—many of whom were stage or literary luminaries—would not be seen on the way out by the next sufferer coming in. This was a wise precaution, since people coming away from a session with Dr. S. usually looked as if they had had fifty minutes on the anvil with an apprentice blacksmith.

Dr. S. was a short, fattish man with very white skin, large dark eyes and a wolfish smile. He described himself—and the grateful, awestruck patients admiringly agreed—as an *enfant terrible* among the conventional psychiatrists. He paid no attention to the psychoanalytic canon that the doctor's relationship with the patient should be detached and impersonal. He played bridge and went to the theater with his patients. Nor did he sit and wait for their confidences. He catechized them with searingly intimate questions—at least, searingly intimate for those days—and if replies were not forthcoming, he said threateningly, "Don't you want to get well?"

His professional knowledge, however, seemed to be limited to discerning sex symbols in everything. Not only were bananas, cigars and frankfurters equated with phalluses, but so were fountain pens, sewer pipes and Oh Henry bars. I once spent three weeks locked in mortal combat with him because I had hung a wreath in the front window for Christmas and he wanted me to admit that the wreath was a symbolic vagina and that I had put it in the window to signal to all male passersby that there was a sexually receptive woman inside.

"Own by owning up to," he used to roar, slapping the arm of his chair.

Since I was the student type, my first impulse on entering analysis was to get some books from the library and read up on the subject, but Dr. S. vetoed this idea out of hand.

"*I'm* your doctor," he barked. "Are you going to listen to sixteen different doctors all at once?"

However, despite his crudities, he had no difficulty in getting a transference from me and it was not long before I was dragging his name into conversations and glowing with a shy and grateful ardor if I heard other people talking about him. I was not one of the patients with whom he socialized, but I went to him six days a week and the hour in his consulting room was the glowing center of my day. All else led up to it or, afterward, trailed with poetic melancholy away.

Nevertheless, for all the swooning accessibility, I had areas of unyielding resistance. An unquestioning disciple of the celebrity culture, Dr. S. had it as his avowed objective to persuade me to go out to Hollywood and swell my bankroll by writing for the movies. It was his idea—and apparently his only idea—of mental health.

Here he found me adamant.

He relied a good deal, in his therapy, on the taunt. "You're afraid," he used to sneer. "You haven't got the guts to go out there."

But he could not get a rise out of me.

However, with so intensive an exposure, it was inevitable that I should be influenced by him. At his direction, I started spending some of the money which had come in from *With Malice*. I had been reared to believe that only weaklings and degenerates go into capital, and the money from the book was, in my view, capital. Dr. S., however, said that this showed I was anal erotic. I was floored by this astonishing view of what I thought was commendable prudence, but since I was already going into capital to pay for the analysis, I went into it further and bought some clothes—not many, but very good. I also developed the reckless habit of taking taxis everywhere (to prove that I was not troubled by retention of stool).

Dr. S. was precipitous and willful, and though I thought of myself as a demure, diffident and biddable character right out of Louisa May Alcott, I was precipitous and willful, too. One day, not long after I had been in analysis, I walked into the doctor's office and told him that I had moved out of the apartment I shared with Henry and that I was going to live by myself for a while until I worked things out.

I did not know what I was going to work out—only that, with no animus at all against Henry, I nevertheless felt trapped by propinquity. Indeed I was trapped, though not by propinquity. The only marriage I had ever seen at close quarters was Reinhold's and Annie's, and from it I had deduced that the single most important thing about a married couple was that there should be no quarrels. What I had not realized was that the even tenor of Henry's and my ways had been achieved at the cost of something very important.

Intimacy.

I was more a household pet than a wife. I could put a paw on Henry's knee, race about with my spaniel ears streaming behind me in a display of enthusiasm or roll over to have my furry stomach rubbed, but emotionally all I could say was "Arf!" If Henry was dissatisfied with the lack of depth in our relationship, he did not say so. Resignation was the key to his character, though I was unable to recognize it, resignation not being a quality existing in large quantities among the Halseys.

Dr. S. was visibly startled and taken aback when I told him I had left home. However, he could not afford to have Henry think that he did not have me under control, and whatever his deficiencies, he could at least turn on a dime. He instantly persuaded himself—and with very little difficulty he persuaded Henry—that this had been part of his plan for me all along.

The next two years were my Lame Duck period. I took up with, in succession, two handsome young men who were very weak and whose lives were in a mess. These lives I proposed, in a passion of reforming zeal, to straighten out. The first young man was an alcoholic and a homosexual. He was subsequently to die of drink at an early age, but at that time he was still holding down a good job, though he was wantonly extravagant and a detached observer would have called him a pathological liar. But I was up to my old childhood pastime of seeing in people what I wanted to see and not what was really there. I was also looking, subconsciously, for some lofty-sounding excuse for not coming to grips with the problem of writing.

At Dr. S.'s suggestion, the young man became a patient of the doctor's and I paid for the treatment. He hated Dr. S. and was always breaking his appointments, but neither the doctor nor I could be deflected. In those days, with Gay Liberation far in the future, being a homosexual was a nightmare of shame, terror and dissimulation. In my ignorance, however—which was shared at the time by the general public—I thought it was just a bit of waywardness on the young man's part which the brisk therapy of Dr. S. would soon dispose of.

I conceived of this rescue mission as one of great nobility on my part, but actually the young man's relationship to me was roughly that of a cracker crumb which is directly in the path of a vacuum cleaner. He did not try to escape, however—partly through alcoholic inertia and partly because I was a screen which, he hoped, would conceal from others and even to some extent from himself his sexual polarity.

After much too long a time and the footing of too many bills, Dr. S. ordered me to break off the association. For once, I complied. I spent a week discovering that it is really true that food can taste like ashes in the mouth, but underneath the anguish, I was secretly relieved. As to the young man, I must for all my mistaken interference in his life have given him at least one moment of pure joy—that being the moment when he realized that somebody had turned off the vacuum cleaner.

The second Lame Duck was a slightly better prospect, being heterosexual and, though a heavy drinker when he could afford it, not an alcoholic. He came from a strict, frugal New England family; had a dishonorable discharge from the Marines for something never fully explained; and was earning a precarious living as a Powers model. I met him right after he had made a suicide attempt, and discovering that his one hopeless yearning in life was to be a commercial pilot, I staked him to flying lessons, gave him a small allowance to live on while he learned and bought him a plane at a cost of two thousand dollars in which to log the necessary hours in the air.

On his record, he was a ne'er-do-well, but for once I saw something in somebody which was really there when no one else saw it. At thirty-two, he was considered too old to learn to fly, and as he had in his school days seen more of the truant officers than the teachers, the mathematics involved were fiendishly difficult for him. But he was grim, dogged and physically courageous and eventually he did qualify as a pilot.

Before that time came, however, I had broken off with him. He lived in a furnished room near the airport where his plane was, and I saw him two evenings a week. Extraordinarily good-looking and a marvelous dancer, he was nevertheless limited, conversationally, to the Gary Cooper "Yup."

So, on the nights when I saw him, we put on evening clothes and went out for dinner and dancing at expensive places. Obviously, I had to pay for these "huge cloudy symbols of a high romance," but Dr. S., who applauded anything I did that cost money, heartily approved of them. It was a far cry from the prudent evenings with the string quartets.

But when Lame Duck No. 2 was about two thirds of the way to his pilot's license, I discovered that he had secretly married a pudgy lady who had a small apartment near the airport and who relieved the tedium of his furnished-room evenings by cooking wonderful dinners for him. He had been married several times before. You just had to lean on him and he would marry you. I did not want to marry him myself, but I felt I had been made a fool of—and by people I regarded as my inferiors, at that.

The lacerating sense of outrage and chagrin was well-nigh unbearable, and I suffered as only those can suffer who mess about with huge cloudy symbols of a high romance. Dr. S.'s helpfulness, incidentally, was limited to giving me a hefty shot of morphine the day I heard the news. The stern but salutary instruction I needed in order to learn something from the experience was completely lacking.

I never saw the second Lame Duck again, but I arranged for him to have the money to finish what he was doing. To do otherwise would simply have wasted what I had already spent. Ultimately, he sold the plane for almost what it cost and returned the money, and when the United States entered World War II, he became one of the civilian pilots who ferried bombers for the Army to the various theaters of war.

What—since I was not writing—did I do with my time in those two years? Both the Lame Ducks were keenly interested in women's clothes and liked the way I wore mine, so many hours were devoted to wandering about in department stores. With the first Lame Duck, I spent a good deal of time

in bars. I did not introduce either of them to my friends. Instead, I hung about with their friends, resolutely concealing
from myself that their friends were a pretty tatty lot. Supposedly—this was Dr. S.'s view—I was being boldly uncon-
ventional and enjoying a freedom I had never had before, but
basically I was scared to death at what I was doing and
haunted by voices that said, "She's no better than she should
be."

I could not have endured the combination of boredom
and fright attendant upon reforming the unreformable, save
that Henry and I were on friendly, affectionate terms and I
had lunch or dinner with him several times a week. It was
understood that the separation was only temporary, while I
lived out or lived through these obsessive high-school-girl
romances. The wayward impulse exhausted, I would return
to Henry's roof. Meantime, he was being "civilized."

How did I get away with it—this thoughtless exploitation
of Henry? How could I have been so unaware that I *was* getting away with something? Will success spoil Rock Hudson?

Success does not implant bad characteristics in people.
It merely steps up the growth rate of the bad characteristics
they already had. I grew up in a household of four people who
shared a dominating pattern of self-concern. When in my
late twenties I suddenly revealed what looked like a considerable money-earning potential, that concern was echoed from
the outside by almost everybody I came in contact with. Not
only was *With Malice* a proppity, I was a proppity myself,
and as such I was treated with reverence and was indulged.
By Henry. By everyone. My conscious objective, very Annie-
ish, was to be thought of as modest and unspoiled, but by
"unspoiled" I meant always being courteous to waiters.

During most of the Lame Duck period, I was unconsciously waiting for Henry to say, "*Achtung!*" And Henry was
not by nature an *Achtung*-sayer. After a while his friends and

relatives began telling him that it was time for him to put his foot down. He must tell me, they said, that if I did not come back, he would get a divorce. But Henry was afraid to risk it. He was afraid I would say, "All right, go ahead and get a divorce." So things hung fire.

It was through Henry himself that I became acquainted with Joseph Bloch. He was a former student of Henry's, eight years my junior, who had been drafted into the Army the summer before Pearl Harbor and who was stationed near New York. Henry had a high opinion of him as an extremely bright but rather disorganized young man who, Henry said, had potentialities as a poet, save that he was unwilling to sit down and do any further work on his promising first drafts. At Henry's suggestion, I sent Corporal Bloch some books. He came to call on me to say thank you and I found him very *simpatico* and asked him back. Soon he was coming to see me whenever he could get away from the Army—which, since America was not yet in the war, was often.

Though he had nice brown eyes, he was short and not particularly good-looking, but after the meaningless symmetry of the tall Lame Ducks, that was rather refreshing than otherwise. In fact, it seemed like a guarantee of probity. A voracious reader, he had a retentive mind and was encyclopedically well-informed. But more than that, he was intellectually manipulative and exploratory. He liked to stand ideas on their heads, to see what they looked like upside down—a trick which C. Wright Mills was later to recommend in one of his books as a very good way of piercing to inner reality.

In the beginning, I was gracious and condescending—the Lady Writer, the Professor's Wife, who was going to offer tea and sympathy to the sensitive young poet immured in the Army. But the sensitive young poet was very relaxed about the Army. The other enlisted men called him

The Brain, and he took care of the company drunks, gave advice to the lovelorn and was very good at card games. Myself about as adaptable as a crowbar, I was fascinated by the pliancy with which he could adjust to any situation in which he found himself.

To someone more worldly-wise than I, he would have been a recognizable type—a young New York Jew, with pogroms not too far back in his family's history, who was fluent, shrewd, resourceful and very, very bright. He differed from the type only in that he lacked ambition. But I had always lacked ambition myself, so it did not seem to me a heinous failing. I had no desire to reform him.

He had, actually, some excuse for not being career-oriented. He had known when he finished college that he was going to be drafted, and he had only had time for a few odd jobs here and there in journalism before being called to the colors. Perhaps it was because he had formed no ties with what would later be called the Establishment that he understood my unwillingness to sell *With Malice* to the movies. A poet *manqué*, he also understood my reluctance to do a rehash of the book.

With this kind of sympathy and support, who needed Dr. S.? I had not known Joseph very long when I told the doctor I was no longer going to be a patient of his. He, upon hearing the news, recoiled. He looked at me like one who, contemplating the raisins on his breakfast cereal, suddenly sees a raisin begin to move. I had not finished my analysis, he said. I would get into trouble without his advice and guidance. I replied that I could no longer afford his fees. He offered to reduce them by half. When I said No, he got argumentative and in the end asked if I would continue coming were he to charge me only a nickel a session. When I still said No, he gave up, and we had a parting which was marked by a certain amount of awkwardness.

And then came an event which dwarfed all personal concerns. Pearl Harbor. Somebody has said that World War II was the last "good" war, and younger people who have only known Korea and Vietnam must find it hard to imagine America engaged in direct, unambiguous conflict with an enemy its own size. But, though it now seems as remote as the Age of Pericles, the national climate during World War II was one of idealism and unquestioning belief in the rightness of the cause. *Dolce et decorum est pro patria mori.* Young men in uniform were everywhere in evidence, and a very popular song at the time was "The Ballad of Roger Young," about an actual G.I. who had saved the lives of four other soldiers by throwing himself on a grenade. Roger Young differed in many important particulars from Lieutenant Calley.

Everybody tried to find something to do for the war effort, and I went to work at the Stage Door Canteen. The Canteen was soon to become famous as the entertainment industry's best-known contribution to the national emergency. Housed in a cramped, low-ceilinged basement on West 44th Street, just off Times Square, it was only for enlisted men. Officers were not admitted.

Nobody talked about "the image" at that time, but the Canteen had one. The newspapers gave it a great deal of publicity as a place where "stars of stage, screen and radio" went faithfully every day to talk to or dance with the servicemen and personally serve them with coffee and sandwiches. Actually, the stars of stage, screen and radio had contracts and commitments which precluded their playing any such romantically humble role day in and day out, though they did show up every once in a while and do their turns on the Canteen's tiny stage.

The day-to-day operation, however, was in the hands of mothers, sisters, wives, cousins and secretaries of people who

were in the performing arts, plus a few men who were 4-Fs
or too old for military service. The Canteen was by no means
the glamour spot the newspapers represented it to be, though
a movie was made called *Stage Door Canteen* which was notable only for songs by Irving Berlin. But it did serve a useful
function, and by the end of the war had been visited by about
three million servicemen.

I had not been there very long when I started, at long
last, to write another book. The war had turned the public
mind—temporarily, at least—away from the cash-and-fame
nexus. I no longer had to feel that people would be watching
quite so alertly (and perhaps maliciously) to see whether I
could duplicate the success of *With Malice*. One day a well-
known lady of the theater who was on the Canteen's board of
directors came in to survey what she clearly regarded as her
private kingdom. Nobody knew what prompted her to say it,
but she looked around and remarked in an all-too-audible
voice, "As soon as I have time, I'm going to clean up this
place and get rid of the Jews."

The entertainment industry in New York has always
contained a high proportion of Jews, so the statement naturally caused a furor among the Canteen workers. The furor
died down, but the little incident constituted one clear call
for me. Since we fought World War II with good consciences
and without the aid of electronics, we had—besides the
heartbreak of the casualty lists—a certain amount of lightheartedness. A bomber squadron in the Pacific had "Hell-
birds' With Malice Toward Some" lettered on its fuselages,
and in 1942 a book called *See Here, Private Hargrove*
swept the country. It was about the Army's basic training program, and it was very funny.

It seemed to me that I could write something amusing
about the home front—the ration books, the shortages and
the phonies who were using the war to advance themselves

personally—and combine it with a serious message. The whole justification for the casualty lists was that we were defending democracy, but "Jewboy" was Standard English for many of the soldiers who came to the Canteen. There seemed to be room for a restatement of what in those days we called "tolerance" for minorities, and if such a restatement could be sugar-coated with humor, it might persuade people who would never dream of reading a tract.

Throughout 1942 and 1943 I worked on the book, maintained an enormous correspondence with servicemen I met at the Canteen and saw a great deal of Joseph. He had been sent for a year to an Army Special Training School at Princeton and came to New York every weekend and sometimes during the week. I had an apartment with high ceilings—it was in an old brownstone—and a wood-burning fireplace. It was charmingly furnished with Victoriana, Victorian furniture having just at that time come back into favor. In front of the crackling logs, we talked avidly—the more avidly because I was at last writing again and working, moreover, at something in whose basic validity both Joseph and I believed completely.

The relationship unrolled like a dropped spool of thread heading for dusty refuge beneath the radiator. Joseph was not familiar with WASPs and at first could hardly believe that this ethnic plum had fallen into his lap. But quick recoveries were his specialty, and he soon discovered that if I was not a born and bred *Yiddisherkopf*, I could at least follow his ideas and produce a few of my own.

For my part, I was not familiar with Jews from a working-class background—Joseph's parents had met at a Socialist picnic—and he seemed to me to have so much vitality, both physical and intellectual, that he made the Simons look languid and overbred. His magnetic attraction for me, however, was that he was the first human being I had ever

trusted enough to talk to at less than arm's length. Because
he was eight years younger than I and therefore not an authority figure? Certainly because he was not afraid of or put
off by my intensity.

The manuscript of the book was at last brought to com-
pletion, and it was Dick Simon again who came up with the
title. He suggested calling it *Some of My Best Friends Are
Soldiers*, though one of the wits at Simon and Schuster nick-
named it "The Handy Vest-Pocket Anti-Prejudicer." Meantime, I had been waiting for my divorce decree to become
final. I had gone back to Henry—though he never did give
me an ultimatum—with Joseph sorrowfully agreeing that it
was the best thing to do. Henry represented security. Without
him, I would be on my own, financially, and despite everyone's positive and reiterated assurances, I had no faith whatever in my ability to keep on earning money by writing.

But I had not been with Henry for a week when I realized that there was nothing ahead in that direction except a
slow withering on the vine. For both of us. And the absent
Joseph exerted a gravitational pull. Nevertheless, it took reso-
lution to decide to marry him. Bourgeois caution had been
instilled into my very bones and Joseph did not have the ear-
marks of a Good Provider. When younger, he had been one
to blow every penny on a present for someone and then
spend the following weeks and months walking everywhere
because he had no carfare. He was no longer quite that
reckless, but since my imagination knew no middle ground, I
could see myself at some future date living like the Terwilligers. However—as I had done when leaving the real estate
company—I blindly obeyed instinct and blocked off thought
of possible consequences.

Having to tell Henry that I wanted a divorce was scarifying. I cannot now remember how the dialogue went on that

portentous occasion, but recall only that I ended by blurting out, "You always come around with your hat in your hand!" He made a sad little gesture of helplessness and went away without saying another word. It was the second time I had pulled freight on somebody I had merely used, but I did not learn the obvious lesson. The obvious lesson was that the only way to prevent the recurrence of such painful scenes was to learn to stand on my own feet and to get over the need to use people.

Joseph and I were married in March of 1944, but did not tell our families until three months later. Joseph's mother and father had a family business in north Jersey which they had just barely managed to pull through the Depression. At the time I met Joseph, however, the business was so prosperous that his parents traveled a lot and were happily experimenting with diamonds, mink and philanthropy.

His father was an extraordinarily homely little man who concealed under chronic grumpiness a good heart and the timidity of a field mouse. His mother was a Jewish matriarch who pressed food without mercy on guests already gorged, but could only nibble on it herself because she always had the bit in her teeth. The little entourage of friends and relatives whom she completely dominated was fond of saying, "Becky would give you the shirt off her back." And it was true. The only trouble was that she neglected to take it off first, and what you found on your back was not only Becky's shirt but Becky too.

Joseph had a brother, and almost as soon as the boys reached the age of puberty, their mother had started trying to marry them off to the kind of girl whom Herman Wouk in *Marjorie Morningstar* called "Shirley from West End Avenue." Becky was furious that her son had contracted a legal matrimonial marriage quite independently of her, but was

compelled to put a good face on it because the entourage was
so much impressed with Joseph's having married what they
called "a famous author."

Joseph treated Becky as a great joke. "I'm the only Jewish boy in New York who isn't afraid of his mother," he said.

I was dazzled by this insouciance, being quite unable to
treat my own parents as a joke. However, remembering Annie's response when I told her I was going to marry Henry, I
was firm with them. I wrote and told them I had remarried,
and said, in effect, that I would bring Joseph up to Newtown
to meet them if they would behave. They did behave. We
went up to Connecticut for a Sunday family dinner, and
Annie and Reinhold surpassed themselves. Annie, for once,
cooked a halfway edible meal and the now aging Reinhold
put himself out—in his old-fashioned, ponderous way—to be
hospitable.

But it was what happened afterward that made the day
memorable. We had no sooner gotten settled on the bus back
to New York than Joseph said, "You've got it all backward.
It's your mother who is the bastard. Your father is a hell of a
guy."

I let out a strangled sound—a kind of yelp—that made
the people sitting near us look at me. In one indescribable
burst of illumination, I saw that he was right. Underneath, I
must have known it all along, because not a syllable of protest rose to my lips. The scales dropped from my eyes about
Annie; and like a fountain being turned on, at first tentatively
and then imperiously, my respect and admiration for Reinhold surged up into awareness. Not that, in that transfiguring
moment, I became any the less afraid of my parents. But
something that was wrong had been set right; the sense of
release was exquisite; and my gratitude to Joseph was almost
more than flesh and blood could support.

When I got home that night, I wrote to my father saying how much I appreciated his having saved money and denied himself things in order to send me to college. Though for years I had treated him with barely concealed impatience as a Victorian fuddy-duddy, he responded to this advance unhesitatingly.

"I was only doing what I wanted to do," he wrote in reply, "and besides, your mother helped."

But while it was good to be reoriented about my parents, this corrective insight was of little use when, shortly thereafter, the Army at long last sent Joseph overseas. Suddenly I had no one on whom to rely for the instant encouragement, praise and reassurance without which I seemed unable to function. As the poet says, I fell upon the thorns of life, I bled. I had always been spaciously ignorant of practical matters. I did not know how to return things to department stores, how to read a contract, whom to call when things broke down or how to put new batteries in a flashlight. And I hugged my ignorance. Tacitly, I blackmailed people into doing things for me by a highly conspicuous display of helplessness.

This was scarcely the ideal equipment for the presumably cheerful and supportive wife of the serviceman overseas. Over and over I tried to remind myself that millions of other women were having to get along without their husbands and that I was luckier than many because I had no children to take care of and Joseph was not in a combat outfit. But these rational and salutary injunctions rolled off my mind like marbles from a tilted platter. Nothing could keep the self-pity out of my letters to Joseph. Reading those letters today, I find some of which I can afford to be proud, as being vivid, brimmingly affectionate and just what a soldier abroad would have liked to receive. But in far too many of them the infantile reproach is unmistakable: You went away. You abandoned me. I blush for those pages today, and would be embarrassed if anyone were to see them.

Two months after Joseph went overseas, and six years after the publication of *With Malice, Some of My Best Friends* came out. An emotionally well-balanced person—into which category very few writers fit—would have been satisfied with its reception. Though the provincial critics bristled and said snarlingly that they did not need me to tell them not to be anti-Semitic, the more sophisticated metropolitan reviewers were generous. The book actually got better notices than it deserved, because it had a broken back. The humorous parts about life on the home front were diverting enough and the exhortations to "tolerance" were ardent, but I had not succeeded in fusing the two. However, nobody seemed to notice this fatal flaw.

Certainly *I* did not notice it. I thought I had written a Deathless Message which would eventually take its place in people's minds and hearts a little below the Gettysburg Address. This kind of delusion is common to writers and is not as ridiculous as might be supposed. After you have put into a book what you have to put into it—have lived with the prospect of exposing yourself in ways you do not even know of to uncaring strangers, have forced the balky mind to take fences it does not want to take, have disciplined yourself like a ballet dancer to nudge the work forward a few paragraphs each day, have ruthlessly deleted all the eloquent bits because they slow the pace, and have brought your stomach back ten thousand times from that nadir to which it sinks when you contemplate your inadequacy—after you have done all that for a period of months or years, how can the result *not* be one of the world's masterpieces?

And what an anguish when it is treated as something immeasurably lower! I remember Mrs. Fisher, when she was in her seventies, speaking with quite uncustomary acidity about a critic who had reviewed one of her books unfavorably thirty years before. No one could have been surer than she of her place in contemporary esteem, but after three decades she still remembered verbatim what that critic had said— remembered and resented it.

With Malice would have been a hard act to follow in any circumstances. To follow it with something that was partly serious and not quite what people were anticipating was simply asking for a certain amount of sour commentary. But I expected universal applause for the goodness of my intentions, and naïvely supposed that my virtuous stance would make me immune from all but the most swallowable criticisms. In addition, I had always had a consuming need to get people to agree with me, and if they stubbornly adhered to what I considered their dangerously wrong opinions, I seethed with rage and despair. Thin-skinned was hardly the word for me, when the second book came out. I made Saint Sebastian with all those arrows in him look like a holiday-maker on a Caribbean cruise.

Pleasant things happened when *Some of My Best Friends* was published, but I barely noticed them. Both Mrs. Roosevelt and Walter Winchell in their respective columns urged their audiences to read the book. Winchell, in fact, made something of a campaign out of it. All I could think of, however, was that NBC canceled a radio dramatization at the last minute as too controversial.

"Do you mean," I said hotly to the bland executive who broke the news, "that there's a *controversy* about whether Christians should behave decently to Jews?"

For a minute he was jolted, but the show was called off nevertheless. Shortly after that Dick Simon characteristically abandoned both the book and me, and this came as a real shocker, even though I should have known it was in the cards. When I detailed these occurrences to Joseph, in heart-rending terms, he wrote wonderfully sustaining letters in reply. But because it was wartime, his letters took weeks to arrive and by the time I received them, I was naked to mine enemies about something else.

Nowadays Americans under pressure gulp tranquilizers until they are like harps strung with boiled spaghetti, but at that time this national habit had not yet taken hold. The only surcease I got from an ever-mounting tension was in alcohol, which I did not lap up convivially in bars, but sipped quietly alone at home in order to get to sleep. The dependence on alcohol did not worry me, because I had a tolerance for liquor that Bacchus himself might have envied and did not know the meaning of the word "hangover." But I sensed that I was heading for some kind of disaster, and the conviction was the more frightening because I could not imagine what form it would take.

I made an effort to cope. At the suggestion of a friend, who said I needed something to take me out of myself, I got a job as teacher's assistant with the small children in a private school. That, plus what I was doing at the Canteen, got me tired enough to sleep at night and my letters to Joseph became more what they should have been. And then in the following April Franklin Roosevelt died.

The Affluent Society and permissiveness have altered people's mental picture of the father figure. Currently, "father figure" means Big Daddy handing out chocolate bars or a blood-drenched Godfather operating as a *deus ex machina*. Whatever the instance, the "child" is passive and the relationship static. But thirty years ago, the father was the one who educated—who brought out people's potential. In both the Depression and World War II, Roosevelt evoked in people qualities they had not known they possessed—resourcefulness, courage and cooperativeness. He himself had conquered powerlessness and helplessness, in his fight against polio, so he insensibly put into people's minds the idea that such conquests were possible.

The death of Roosevelt plunged the nation into a grief that has not been paralleled since, because he was the next-to-the-last President whose "children" were supposed to be active, not passive. What the sudden loss of that father figure meant in my own psychic scheme of things I was quickly to find out. The day after the President died, I was riding in the subway on my way to the school when, between one second and the next, I was struck by such abject physical terror that only by clenching my teeth and calling on every ounce of Reinhold-type willpower did I manage to keep from fainting. The disaster of which I had had a premonition had caught up with me. Agoraphobia.

Words cannot convey the intensity of phobic terror. It is no mere formless apprehension—no vague malaise which can be thrown off by resolute effort. One is pulverized with fear. The knees buckle, hands and forehead are drenched in sweat, the parched mouth is sandpaper and great swimming waves of panic dim the vision. The sensation is one of utter helplessness against a huge and implacable menace which is going to annihilate you before you draw your next breath.

There is no facing up to this nameless immensity of peril because it cannot be located. Sometimes it seems to be coming from above and behind. Sometimes it comes in from all around, from every quarter of the compass. The psychiatrists—in what must be the classic understatement of all time—call this shattering phenomenon "anxiety." It would take a Kafka to delineate it. Lacking a Kafka, one can only describe it as the total absence of safety.

I did not have this "anxiety" if I was riding in a taxi, nor did I have it if someone accompanied me. But I could not venture out of my house alone, even to go to the corner to mail a letter, without being reduced to a subhuman pulp. The school was too far away to be reached by taxi, so I had to give up the job there, and there seemed no option but another venture into psychoanalysis. Dr. B., to whom I went this time, was an elderly man, very sweet and gentle, who had been analyzed by Freud and who stood high in psychoanalytic circles in New York.

The people I knew were enlightened and not the sort who say impatiently to phobia victims, "It's all in your mind. Just pull yourself together." Nevertheless, I was desperately ashamed of this affliction and would not tell anyone about it if there were any possible way to avoid telling them. I made up my mind that I would not permit the phobia to alter my way of life, and if there was no one to go with me, I forced myself to go out alone. I was more dead than alive when I got into a "safe" place again, but it was preferable to staying at home and thus tacitly acknowledging the sovereignty of the phobia.

"It's serious," said Dr. B. "It will take a long time to get over it."

He was more prescient than he knew. It was to be eleven years—and I had long left Dr. B. behind—before I could once again walk out of my house alone as carelessly as I had formerly done. Not once during those years did I entertain for a split second the idea of acceptance—of resigning myself to this limitation and learning to live with it gracefully. I used to set myself exercises.

"Today I will walk a block alone. Tomorrow I will walk a block and a half."

In the spring of 1945, however, I had no idea of what lay ahead and since I was not going to the school, it seemed as if the best use to which I could put my time would be to write another book. This time there would be no broken back. I was going to forget about the cap and bells and be an out-and-out reformer.

5

Fresh Woods,
and Pastures New

World War II may have been a "better" war than Vietnam, but at that time black servicemen were in all-black units and the U.S.O. had separate recreational facilities for them. Or, in some cases, no provision for them at all. Theater people, however, were traditionally less prejudiced than the general public, and the Stage Door Canteen was one of only two canteens in the entire country which was open to black servicemen as well as white. That was not why I went there. I only discovered the Canteen's biracial setup after my arrival, but I kindled to the idea immediately and was soon asked to serve on the Race Relations Committee. In the spring of 1945, I started writing *Color Blind*, which grew out of my experiences on that committee.

In the last thirty years, so much has happened of both good and bad vis-à-vis race that the situation of a generation ago now seems, if one may use the word, quaint. The Canteen's Race Relations Committee had been formed out of necessity, because the climate of the times was so unenlightened that the Red Cross even segregated the blood plasma. Hence it was not enough simply to open the doors to black servicemen. That was done; but after they came in, they stayed together—tentative lookers-on—in a corner. The Race Relations Committee came into existence for the purpose of getting the black soldiers distributed evenly throughout the room.

In those days what Caucasians called "the Negro problem" was by tacit agreement swept under the rug. White liberals—a term which had not yet become opprobrious— usually ended their discussions of it with the comfortably dismissive phrase, "It's all a matter of education." Used in this sense, "education" meant changing white public opinion, but nobody ever specified who was going to do this educating, or where, or how. The Race Relations Committee, however, actually did just such a job.

The people who had to be educated were the young women who acted as hostesses. There were about a thousand of them—mostly white, but a few black—and because of unsettled wartime conditions, there was a high turnover. We interviewed them; we circulated memoranda; we held special meetings to remind them that they were supposed to make all the servicemen welcome and not just the white ones. We tried to give them enough background and information so that they would really want to do so. By War Department order, the girls at the Canteen were not allowed to make dates with the servicemen they met there, for fear that their ranks might include a few enemy spies looking for news of troop movements. Nobody, therefore, was going to get into deep water unless she asked for it by breaking the rules.

The hostesses were young, and some of them became enthusiastic converts. Others went along—with reservations—because we had something they wanted. We had men, tons of young men, and we only permitted access to them on our terms. There were plenty of all-white entertainment centers where the white hostesses could do their bit, if

that was the arrangement they preferred, but the Stage Door
Canteen was the one that had the most prestige.

As a matter of fact, I got rather arbitrarily educated
myself, when I first went to work on that Committee. I had a
romantic notion—based on complete lack of contact with
them—about the Wonderful Oppressed. I thought that sys-
tematic oppression had the effect of making the victims
saintly, and was startled to discover that some black people
played on the white person's sense of guilt to secure advantages for themselves to which they were not entitled.

Also, there was a social hierarchy in the black community of those days whereby light-skinned blacks were considered much more attractive than very dark-skinned ones. We
sometimes had to reprimand a *café au lait* hostess for being
unwilling to dance with soldiers who were very dark. The af-
firmation of more recent years, that black is beautiful, is not
reverse racism, but was in its inception a much-needed corrective.

And how did the white servicemen react, suddenly presented with the spectacle of white girls dancing with black
men? In those days, we did not use the word "confronta-
tion." We used the vaguer word "trouble." We were able to
avoid "trouble" at the Canteen because the military had a
rule that men in uniform had to stand at attention whenever
"The Star-Spangled Banner" was played. This gave whoever
was in charge a chance to have someone telephone the
M.P.s or the Shore Patrol, who were based only a stone's
throw away. We always had the national anthem at the
ready, but during the four years the Canteen was in operation, it was only played twice, and only once because of a
disturbance about race.

A few white servicemen came in, took one look, and
stamped out—pausing only to spit out the information that
where they came from, it only cost thirty-five dollars to kill

the bastards. A little more frequently, they would buttonhole the nearest person who looked responsible and embark on an oration about—can anyone believe it today?—big black bucks and pure white Southern womanhood. The slightly more sophisticated would sometimes argue long and earnestly with those hostesses who felt disposed to defend the arrangement. But for the most part, the white servicemen accepted it. It was a *fait accompli*, and they were only passing through.

At the Canteen, as in so many other instances, I was indebted to Joseph for putting me on the right track right from the start. When I first encountered Negrophobe soldiers, I used to harangue them, trying to make them feel guilty and, it must be admitted, deliciously aware of the superiority of my own moral position.

The first time I started describing one of these encounters to Joseph, he cut me short abruptly.

"You only make things worse for black people," he said, "when you talk to the white boys like that."

I stared at him.

"When those white soldiers go back to their little Southern towns," he said, "they're going to bear down even harder on the blacks because of your having called them Fascist bigots."

I felt the pedestal on which I had placed myself buckle beneath me, and that is one of the most piercingly humiliating sensations that flesh is heir to—the bolt-of-lightning transition from preening self-approval to the chagrin of having been shown up to be wrong. But the force of Joseph's argument could not be denied.

"If you want to change their minds," he added, "you have to give them an out for their ego."

From then on I tried to persuade instead of to hector, but I was nevertheless frightened the whole time I worked on the Race Relations Committee—at least, when I was on the

floor of the Canteen. And so, I believe, were the others who
shared responsibility for the no-discrimination policy. There
had been a horrifying race riot in Detroit in 1942—or rather,
a three-day massacre of black people by trigger-happy
whites—and we were aware of the latent explosiveness in the
situation we had set up. Although those were not violent
times, two black lieutenants were beaten up one night just
down the street from the Canteen; and as late as 1948, General Eisenhower, testifying before Congress, advised that the
Air Force should be kept segregated because, he said, you
cannot legislate about people's feelings.

We were constantly reminded of how saturated with
prejudice the social fabric was. Sometimes white and black
hostesses at the Canteen would get friendly with each other
and want to go out somewhere, after we had shut up shop,
for coffee and cake. But the Canteen was on West 44th
Street, and the nearest place where whites and blacks could
eat together without problems was Harlem. There was a New
York State law which forbade restaurateurs to refuse service
to anyone because of race, but the law did not specify *when*
you were to be served if some of your number were black, so
the usual practice was to keep black people waiting an hour
or more before taking their order.

There was only one restaurant where we could eat
together comfortably, and that was a little place on the West
Side over by the docks which was frequented by stevedores
and out-of-work actors. This place was so unappetizing that
we always referred to it as the Running Sore Grill, but they
served us promptly.

We were almost all women, on the Race Relations
Committee, and all of us always maintained an outward pre-
tense that what we were doing was simply the normal and obvious thing to do. By no stretch of the imagination could we

have been called militants. We dreaded being challenged, and when we were, most of us did not respond with aplomb. We were apt to lick dry lips and be a bit too nervously placating. But we believed in what we were doing—and there was no denying that the thing worked.

I was impelled to write *Color Blind* because when the war was over, the Canteen would go out of existence. It therefore seemed as if somebody ought to set down the record of its experience so that other people who might want to do something similar in peacetime would be encouraged to try. It was for the Guns of Navarone to write the big novels exploring in depth the white man's guilt. All I could do was a straightforward account of the Peaceable Kingdom near Times Square on the simple basis that "I was there, and this is how it seemed to me."

It was while I was at home working on the book that I got as bad a jolt of fright as any I had ever experienced with infuriated racists at the Canteen. I was standing at the window one day—standing at the window is how writers get most of their work done—when I suddenly realized that if I did not include in *Color Blind* a chapter called "How Would You Like Your Daughter to Marry One?" I would not have an honest book. I was appalled. That question had even the best-intentioned white people backed into corners, red-faced and stammering. I had coped with it often enough on a person-to-person basis at the Canteen, but to tackle it publicly, in a book which had to run the gauntlet of reviewers, was going out of the way to seek a martyr's crown.

Sober studies like Gunnar Myrdal's *An American Dilemma*, published in 1944, had shown that black people wanted equality of opportunity and were not interested in intermarriage, and it seemed fairly obvious that by the time interracial marriages became a commonplace, we would all

have made the necessary adjustments to the idea. The difficulty, however, was that white people did not really look
forward with any relish to such adjustments being made.

Today we have a climate of sexual permissiveness and
there is no longer any such thing as forbidden fruit, but a
generation ago, there were so few contacts between blacks
and whites, except on the Yassuh-boss level, that the black
man was an unknown quantity and white people's sexual
imaginings about him made the sewers of Paris look like an
operating theater. Nevertheless, if I sidestepped the question
of intermarriage, I would have a book that, in its very evasiveness, subtly confirmed prejudice. I decided to grasp the
nettle, but I could only nerve myself to go ahead by thinking
of the old British naval maxim, "When in doubt, steer for
the sound of the guns."

I need not have worried. When *Color Blind* came out in
1946, it was a success. Not with the same set of people who
had bought *With Malice*. And not with so many. But the
decision to include the chapter on "How Would You Like,
etc." proved to have been the right one. That chapter and a
companion one called "Sex, Jealousy and the Negro" seemed
to have a liberating effect and relieve a good deal of anxiety,
and the publishers collected so many endorsements from an-
thropologists, ministers, community leaders and even Clare
Boothe Luce that they had to put an extra flap on the book's
jacket to accommodate them.

Naturally, not everybody took *Color Blind* to their bo-
soms. Some bookstores in the South refused to stock it, and
some years later, during the McCarthy period, it was re-
moved from several public libraries on the grounds that it was
obscene. Orville Prescott, for many years literary critic of *The
New York Times*, remarked to Dick Simon that it was the
most irritating book he had ever read, and William
Faulkner—applied to by the publishers for a blurb—wrote

them an immensely long and turgid letter which he concluded by saying, "It's all very well, but you can't overlook
Pickett's Charge." However, N.A.A.C.P. chapters throughout the country ordered thirty or so copies at a time. (The
N.A.A.C.P in those days was considered very radical.) The
book also got a book club selection, was given an award by an
organization called the Council Against Intolerance, and was
put into a few college courses as required reading.

With the publication of *Color Blind*, I had completed a
seemingly eccentric trajectory from entertainer to reformer.
But it was only seemingly eccentric. *With Malice* had been
the ebullient production of my youth, and to have continued
in that vein would have been, in effect, an attempt to
prolong youth for three or four decades beyond its natural
termination. It could have been done. The ebullience could
have been faked, and I would probably have made a lot of
money from it. But merely thinking about the idea made me
feel exhausted.

In writing *Color Blind*, I was reverting to type. *With
Malice* had cast me in the role of court jester, but when I was
attending P.S. 21 in Lincoln Park, we used to recite a poem
called "The Fool's Prayer" about a court jester who was ordered by a mocking king to compose an extemporaneous
prayer. Two lines of this effusion made a strong impression
on me.

> They could not see the bitter smile
> Beneath the painted grin he wore.

I did not want to be a court jester, because a court jester is by
definition a courtier—and whatever else the modest purlieus
of Lincoln Park may have been, in the years between 1910
and 1920, they were definitely republican-with-a-small-*r*.

Equally definitely, they were Protestant. Thomas Mann
in *Buddenbrooks* says of one of his characters, "He was at

bottom none the less the born Protestant: full of the true Protestant's passionate, relentless sense of personal responsibility." The sense of personal responsibility I unquestionably had. I wore the woes of the world on my shoulders like epaulettes.

Such epaulettes are not exactly the shortest road to universal popularity. Reformers, crusaders and do-gooders are always being accused of acting from egotistic motives—of simply wanting to feel morally superior. So far as I was concerned, there was truth in the accusation. Egotism had figured largely in my ministrations to the Lame Ducks, and later on, when I transferred my zeal for improvement to a larger field, I certainly took an unacknowledged pleasure in feeling morally superior to the heathen in his blindness.

But the second charge which is always leveled against the bleeding hearts and the uplifters—that they are refusing to face reality—is less valid. The people who say that you are not facing reality actually mean that you are not facing *their idea* of reality. Reality is above all else a variable, and nobody is qualified to say that he or she knows exactly what it is. As a matter of fact, with a firm enough commitment, you can sometimes create a reality which did not exist before. Protestantism itself is proof of that.

By the time *Color Blind* was published, the war was over and Joseph had come home. Oddly enough, our reunion was not ecstatic. At first we were awkward and strange with each other. The articulateness which had been so marked in our courtship and overseas correspondence seemed to fall on its face when we were actually living together full time, and there was a dismaying period when we were each afraid to say to the other, "Have we made a terrible mistake?"

Joseph, in addition, had the problem of what—after five

and a half years in the Army—he should do to earn a living. Because he was inventive, and had a genius for thinking up quirky or inspired slogans, people urged him to go into advertising, which was at that time still considered a glamorous career.

I blew cold on the idea.

"The minstrel boy to the wars has gone,
    In the ranks of Dreft you will find him,"

I said. In all seriousness, I thought he would be a misfit among the hucksters. They were required by the exigencies of their calling to make wit and facetiousness a substitute for honor. For all Joseph's liveliness of mind, he did not have a single grain of facetiousness in him, so he would have been stuck with honor. As he was already stuck with a strong-minded wife, Madison Avenue did not seem the right place for him.

Eventually, he went into the field of education, taking an administrative job at a large school in New York City. The head of the school, Angus Cotter, had been a friend of mine for years. Dedicated to his calling and universally respected and beloved, Dr. Cotter was a man capable of inspiring people, and Joseph seemed to have no regrets for the larger emoluments of advertising. He had what is known as job satisfaction—though there ought to be some less pedestrian phrase for describing what is in its actuality so far from being pedestrian. And he not only got satisfaction, he gave it. After he had been in his job for a while, Dr. Cotter wrote me a letter thanking me for having sent his way so valuable a person as Joseph Bloch.

And our marriage—after the wobbly period of getting reconditioned to peacetime life—seemed to come into its own. I, it turned out, was one of the nest-building Halseys.

Abandoning my previous scorn and contempt for domestic
tasks, I threw myself into the business of running a comfortable household.

> Bed and jug and candle,
> In Agamemnon's house and in Iseult's,

summed up my altered view.

Moreover, now that my dependence was no longer subject to the strain of separation, I could always make Joseph
laugh. He was stockily built, and after I learned to cook, he
began to put on weight. Surveying himself in the mirror one
day, he said mournfully, "I'm just a short fat American."

"No such thing," I replied promptly. "You're a tall lean
teddy bear."

Unlike his wife, Joseph was at bottom profoundly pes-
simistic. He would never discuss how he felt about being
Jewish, but at the core of his nature was the permanent, in-
ternalized weeping of the ghettoized, and more than most
people, he needed gaiety in his life.

As a matter of fact, with both my husbands I always had
one thing going for me. They were both people who loved
their native tongue. They both had the same feeling for the
English language that Dionysius had for the grape, and with
persons like that, the piercing phrase—the command of a vocabulary—is practically an aphrodisiac and compensates for
many staring defects of character.

The staring defects were there, however. After *Some of
My Best Friends* came out—when I was spinning around
emotionally like a cork in a churn—a friend had suggested
that I should take a Rorschach test. I did, and the woman
who interpreted the results said that I had a fine grasp of abstract concepts, but also a towering egocentricity.

"Towering" was the word she used, and it struck me so

squarely between the eyes that all protests about how nice I was to people died a-borning. Later on—when the war was over and my personality was subjected, with Joseph, to the test of genuine intimacy—it became apparent that I *had* been spoiled by the success of my first book. In the outside world I was still as starchy as a clergyman's collar, but at home I was the uninhibited prima donna.

I remember one evening when we were going out to dinner and Joseph had said he would bring me home a black belt. The cleaner had lost the one for the dress I was planning to wear, and when I looked out of the window, after Joseph had left for the office in the morning, I quailed at the prospect of going out by myself to get another one. The terror of being alone in the streets was too much to face, so I phoned Joseph and asked if he could get me a black belt during his lunch hour.

He came in after work and tossed a package on the coffee table.

"There you are," he said. "Mission accomplished."

I opened the package, stared at the contents, and then looked up at him aghast.

"It's brown," I said in a hollow voice.

"Isn't that what you wanted?"

"I said black. I specifically told you black."

Joseph spoke cheerfully. "Can't you wear it anyway?"

"Wear a *brown* belt with a black print?"

"I'm sorry, honey. I was rushed at lunchtime and I thought you said brown. Can't you wear a different dress?"

"But this is the dress I planned to wear!"

With the air of one who has hit upon a happy solution, Joseph asked, "Couldn't you wear it without a belt?"

I made no answer, allowing an eloquent silence to convey the palpable absurdity of such an idea. Dress, in those days, was not so casual as it has since become.

"Maybe you've got a ribbon or something you could tie around your waist for a sash."

"Who do you think I am? Kate Greenaway?"

He pursed his lips judicially. "What about the woman upstairs? She might have a belt you could borrow."

"She isn't home," I said, not without relish.

Joseph nodded to himself, went into the hall and came back with his coat on. "The little notion store down the street might still be open."

When he came back, in a very few minutes, I was in the bedroom. All my clothes from the closet were on the bed and the open dresser drawers looked as if a customs official had been going through them for illicit diamonds.

Joseph was, of course, empty-handed.

"You go without me," I said tragically. "Tell them I have a cold or something."

"Darling, trust me, it's not all that bad."

"But I'd set my heart on wearing that dress!"

"This is a big city," Joseph said, "and we have friends here. There must be somebody we could call up. We could take a taxi and pick up the belt on the way."

This not being an abstract concept, I failed signally to grasp it.

"It might be wrong for the dress. Besides, there's nobody my size."

A trace of complacency here, for I prided myself in those days on having a small waist.

Joseph picked up a dress from the bed. "You look lovely in this one."

"The neck has to be fixed. It would take an hour."

This was not true, but I was not, at the moment, quite so hot in pursuit of eternal verities as I had been when I was writing *Color Blind*.

"I counted on you!"

The tone—a delicate approximation of woman wailing for her demon lover—was intended to shatter Joseph's equanimity.

In that, it did not succeed. He picked up another dress and looked at it thoughtfully.

"That! Everybody hates me in that. I don't know why I bought it."

Had I been in a mood for unsparing self-scrutiny, I might have realized that I was humiliated because the phobia had prevented me from going out and getting the belt myself, and trying to make Joseph feel abject seemed the only way to rebuild self-esteem. He, however, appeared to be standing up to the pressure.

The dialogue went on for some time, with me saying things like, "It's not so much to ask—just that you should pay a little bit of attention to what I say," while he was goodnaturedly persuasive and did not remind me that he had been asked to give up part of his lunch hour.

At length he turned me so that I was facing the full-length mirror, and standing behind me, reached for a dress from the bed. This he held up on me as women do when they take a garment from the rack in a store.

"You can't say nobody liked you in this. Everybody raved about it."

Looking in the mirror, I saw Joseph's face behind my own reflection, and suddenly the need to be obstructionist vanished and I realized the figure I had been cutting.

"I'm sorry," I said contritely.

"The princess and the pea," he remarked wryly, and then gave me a dismissive slap on the fanny and added in a brisk voice, "Get going. We haven't much time."

Why would any man in his right senses want to lumber himself with a child bride like the foregoing? Actually, it was the abstract concepts that saved my bacon. "Love," said

Saint-Exupéry, "does not consist of looking into each other's eyes, but of looking outward together in the same direction." When I was not being a prima donna, Joseph and I shared completely certain basic attitudes, and one of the most important of them was that we did not want to live submerged in the present. We wanted a three-dimensional life—one which included an awareness of the past and a certain amount of prescience about the future.

In the fall of 1948, as a matter of fact, I turned out to be as prescient as your friendly neighborhood sibyl, because I said Harry Truman was going to win the Presidential election. Our friends mopped the floor with me. "The men in white coats will be coming along for *you*," was their most charitable comment. Even Joseph, who always professed great respect for my intuitions, thought I was hallucinating. But I had heard Mr. Truman and his daughter on the radio when they did their whistle-stop campaign, and had been impressed by their unpretentiousness and the unobtrusive courage with which they faced certain defeat. I thought that what I felt, others would feel, too.

Besides wanting to live the three-dimensional life, Joseph and I also shared a considerable impatience—not to abate with the passing years—with what seemed to us the faddishness of supposedly enlightened opinion in the United States. Educated and liberal people would get hold of a word—"dichotomy" or "viable" or, later on, "parameter" or "infrastructure"—and use it for six months so continuously that you began to gag when you heard it, and then suddenly they got tired of it and it dropped out of the language.

There seemed, too, to be evanescent intellectual fashions about ideas. When Eisenhower was President, the seal-sleek political pundits kept saying over and over again that the American Presidency had become too big a job for one man. However, as soon as John F. Kennedy was elected, this

particular formulation—believed at the time to be a great political insight—vanished like a scruple from Richard Nixon's
mind.

Pamela Hansford Johnson once said that the greatest
part of marriage is talk—that the more you have to talk
about, the longer it is going to last. Except when we were
sulking or being haughty after a quarrel, there was never a
moment when Joseph and I could not find anything to say to
each other. We were lucky, too, in that the good auspices
under which he had started his job did not prove to be decep-
tive. He had a fruitful and productive relationship with Dr.
Cotter—who was to him very much the father he wished his
own father had been—and he had respect for the work he
was doing. This was important, for even back in the years
right after the war, there was beginning to be a certain
amount of *angst* about some of the ways in which people
earned a living.

We both of us felt it to be important to what I might call
the resonance of our marriage that we had ties with members
of the preceding generation for whom we had a high regard.
We went to Vermont twice a year to visit Mrs. Fisher and to
Newtown twice a month to see my father, who was slowly
but inexorably coming to the end of his span. Mrs. Fisher's
only son had been killed in the war, and she wrote to me
after one of our visits, "Joseph is a perfect joy for an old
woman who has lost her son. He is the embodiment of vitality and intelligence and good will."

When we went to Newtown, we had long political discussions with Reinhold, who had voted for Roosevelt in
1932, but quickly thereafter began calling him "that man in
the White House." Age, however, had not impaired his
streak of intellectual honesty and Joseph—a deft maneuverer
in social situations—used to peel attitudes off him as you
would take layers off an onion. By the end of the evening my

father would be talking like the young man he had once been whose hero was Eugene V. Debs.

Annie would never join in these conversations, though we urged her and promised not to talk politics. She always busied herself with something about the house, coming to the door of the living room every once in a while to look in and say scornfully, "Talk! Talk! Talk!" It was pathetic, but there was nothing one could do about it. Reinhold, on the other hand, used to say, "Joseph is the kind of son-in-law to have."

Joseph's and my relationship seemed to have an admirable equilibrium; but through the phobia, indirectly, I became aware that despite the apparently enviable community of feelings and attitudes, there was a disruptive element present and the disruptive element was me. It was like something showing up on a kind of interior radar screen—the feeling that this second marriage was not going to last, any more than had the first, unless I did something about myself. In three years with Dr. B., the doctor talked Oedipus until the cows came home, but it did not have the slightest effect on my terror of going out of the house by myself. However, when I stopped going to him, Joseph suggested that I should keep a diary and try to continue the analysis by myself.

Or, rather, with him. I kept the diary and we went over the pages together, discussing and dissecting and trying to find some key that would let me out of the prison of phobic terror. We did not find one, and before long I gave up analyzing dreams and trying to probe the murky depths of the subconscious and concentrated instead on recording, with a view to improving it, my everyday behavior—particularly toward Joseph.

One of the things that made me difficult to have around the house was a ruthless perfectionism, and I remember with perfect clarity the day that I got a sudden and liberating insight into that particular compulsion. I was lying on the sofa, totally exhausted from cleaning the house (which had not really needed it) in a fashion that made Hercules in the Augean stables look like a broken reed. Suddenly I became aware that everything I did was done, not in relation to the needs of other human beings—though I pretended it was—but in relation to an Invisible Critic.

This Invisible Critic inhabited a corner of the room, up near the ceiling, and I unconsciously expected, whenever I had completed a task, to hear a loud, clear voice saying from the corner of the ceiling, "Margaret Halsey, that's the best goddamned mayonnaise that any woman has ever made." Of course, no such voice ever made itself heard, but I never gave up hope, and what chronic, unassuageable tension that unrecognized hope generated!

I kept the diary, on and off, for a period of about ten years, and always with the purpose of bending back, a sixty-fourth of an inch at a time, the talons my parents had buried in me when I was a child. My mother, the *ersatz* Lady Prioress, had always treated me as an extension of herself, and four decades later, if Joseph was running the vacuum, I was on tenterhooks for fear he would not do it exactly the way I would have. To keep silent and let him do things his way instead of mine gave me intense anxiety. What if he botched the job? In my parents' ambience, when I was a child, botched jobs were given very short shrift, and short shrift had come to be, in my view, the prevailing climate of the universe.

The talons my parents had sunk in me did not retract like the landing gear on a plane. Reinhold's nonretractable talon was the need always to be in control of events. This involved making plans, which then became as unalterable as the laws of the Medes and the Persians, to cover every possible contingency.

"Let things happen," Joseph used to say.

My years in high school and college had been a period of slowly dissolving ignorance, and the long years of my marriage were also a time of slowly dissolving ignorance. But my ignorance as a young person about the Victorian novel and the law of diminishing returns was highly soluble, whereas my ignorance about the kind of person I really was, was not.

Insight is one thing. To act upon it—to change one's self in accordance with it—is something else again. Writers in particular have a panic fear that any alteration of the personality structure—however seemingly desirable—will destroy the ability to write. But one of the basic tenets of White Anglo-Saxon Protestantism is a belief in the perfectibility of human beings. Moreover, the phobic terror was in its way a blessing in disguise, for without that tremendous Nay being said to me whenever I wanted to move about freely, I would never have had the incentive to try to sort myself out.

In 1948, Joseph and I clocked off the most significant milestone of all, for in that year we adopted a baby girl, it having turned out that I could not have children. The adoption was arranged before she was born. She was premature, and had to spend three weeks in an incubator, but we got her right from the hospital. We called her Celia. She was a pretty baby, and healthy, though she weighed only five pounds when she was first put into my arms.

"Oh, you *darling!*" I said in that ineffable moment and she smiled at me.

A five-pound baby is so small as to be just barely visible to the naked eye and when we brought her home, I sat up all night the first night watching her for fear she would stop breathing. The Visiting Nurse who came in the next day laughed when she saw the circles under my eyes.

"All babies are tough," she said, "and this one is

tougher than most"—a judgment which, many years later, was to prove most fortunately accurate.

Joseph's mother had eleven brothers and sisters, all still alive and all but one of them with families, and as they were a very clannish lot, Joseph had had a good deal of experience in taking care of children. It was no trouble to him to share in the routines of feeding, changing diapers and making formula, and this was a profound satisfaction. Not because I found the routines onerous. On the contrary, they seemed to me a privilege. But because taking joint care of Celia seemed to bring her father and me together in a kind of mutuality that went deeper than anything we had ever experienced before.

Joseph was, so to speak, a seasoned campaigner; but I had hardly ever seen a baby from any closer than across the room and Celia touched and moved me at depths I had not known I possessed. It was not only the evocation of tenderness and protectiveness—the Girl in the Glacier disappearing in one final mellifluous gurgle. I was also suffused with a feeling to which people nowadays are not very much subject.

Wonder.

When, some years later, we Americans put a man on the moon, it seemed to me the dullest thing since Victor Hugo. We stained the white radiance of eternity with astronauts saying, "A-Okay"—besides spending money for which there was a crying need right here on earth. But what gave me the "What-hath-God-wrought?" feeling was that our daughter, minute as she was, actually had fingernails and could yawn. Had anyone said to me, scoffingly, that you would think no baby had ever been born before, I would have opened my eyes very wide and said, "Oh? Has one been?"

Our daughter put on weight; the slate-gray eyes she had

had at birth turned to a velvety brown; and her silky cap of
fine straight hair metamorphosed into ambrosial ringlets. As
time passed and she got beyond infancy, Joseph turned out to
be much better than I at amusing her. He could invent
games and make up imaginative stories, whereas my stories
always ground to a lumbering halt after the first paragraph.
But I was the one who did the analytical thinking about par-
enthood.

This was not because I had more vision than Joseph, but
because he had to spend all day at the school, thinking about
his job, and when he came home in the evening, he and his
daughter—especially when she got past babyhood—had an
ongoing love affair that made Tristan and Isolde look like a
divinity student holding hands with a female Prohibitionist.
It was at my hardheaded instigation, therefore, that after
Celia was born, we visited Joseph's family quite regularly—
usually about once a week.

Joseph was casual about his parents and had it been left
to him, we would not have seen much of them. But—
although nobody at that time was talking about the nuclear
family—it seemed to me that the tiny unit of Joseph and
Celia and me would be too intense an environment for our
daughter and ought to be diluted. By the time Celia was
born, Reinhold's arteries were hardening and he was too frail
to be much of a grandparent. Joseph's mother, on the other
hand, was still in her perdurable prime and at first glimpse of
Celia had exclaimed, "She's a mensch! She's a little
mensch!"

My mother-in-law was family conscious to such a degree that if she had a mere four or six kinfolk at her table, she
thought she was in solitary. We were so tightly packed in at
that groaning board that I used to say it took three days, after
one of Becky's family dinners, to get back the use of your el-
bows. They were lively meals, however. The one bachelor

uncle was a dyed-in-the-wool reactionary and all the rest were liberals, so what took place on these occasions was a sort of political Hare and Hounds.

Celia was my mother-in-law's only grandchild and likely to remain so, as Joseph's brother lived with his parents and showed no disposition to marry. From the very first, Becky and Celia had a mutually satisfactory relationship and it was pleasant to see them together. When she was a little girl, however, Celia once said, "Grandma doesn't listen." And indeed, she did not. Sometimes, when I was telling her some little incident that I thought she might find entertaining, she would interrupt me in mid-sentence to say reflectively, "I'm having the Weissmans to dinner next week and I can't think what to serve for canapés." I never could decide whether to plow ahead with my story like a sort of conversational Sherman tank or to let the poor little thing be aborted in mid-career.

Aside from this disconcerting habit, however, Becky was very polite to me, as I was to her. On my part, it was appeasement, for I was afraid of her and always used Joseph as a stalking-horse when it was a question of telling her that—despite her never-say-die representations—we were not going to somebody's *bar mitzvah*. It was she, rather than Joseph's father, who really ran the family business and she was highly successful at it. For that very reason, however, something told me that, were things ever to get down to the nitty-gritty, it would turn out that the way she understood the rules of the game was not the way I understood them. (And, of course, I took it for granted that the way I understood them was the right way.) But there seemed no reason why things should ever get down to the nitty-gritty, and in the meantime I was grateful to her for supplying Celia, as I could not, with an extended family.

They were halcyon years, those revolving seasons when

Celia was growing up, and to me, it was a source of recurrent wonderment and abiding satisfaction that the little household of Celia and Joseph and me had everything the Reinhold-and-Annie menage had lacked—family jokes, cosiness, trust and even a pair of Siamese cats who had a most-favored-nation treaty which they enforced down to the last comma. But we were not living in a cocoon, though it sometimes, delightfully, seemed that way. In the outside world, harsh winds were beginning to blow.

6
Not in Front
of the Children

In 1948, the year Celia was born, the Hiss case burst into the headlines, where it was to stay for a long time, and all through the late forties and early fifties my diary is full of references to the ominous turn that American life was taking.

"The dangerous and corrupting hysteria about communism . . ."

"A culture seemingly bent on suicide . . ."

"The pressure on the American middle class to forget it ever heard of morality . . ."

"The anti-Communist prating about 'loyalty' to the government is idiotic. Loyalty has to be a two-way street. The citizens must be loyal to their government, but equally the government must be loyal to the citizens and protect their rights. A government cannot demand loyalty; it has to earn it."

In the spring of 1949, I felt it incumbent on me—not to stand up and be counted—but to sit down and not be counted. An organization called the Independent Citizens Committee for the Arts, Sciences and Professions had scheduled a conference at the Waldorf. The I.C.C. had been formed during World War II for the purpose of integrating

artists and intellectuals into the war effort, and all of us at the
Stage Door Canteen had joined it as a matter of course,
though I had never gone to a meeting or taken any interest in
it.

A few days before its Waldorf Conference was supposed
to begin, there was a sudden outcry that the I.C.C. was
Communist-dominated. Immediately there appeared on the
front page of *The Herald Tribune* a whole collection of letters
from prestigious intellectuals—former members of the
I.C.C.—denouncing the conference and proclaiming the
writers' hatred of Communism. In one day, half a dozen
people, none of whom I knew, telephoned me and warned
me to hurry up and get my letter into the *Tribune*.

But I looked at the letters that had been printed and
knew that I could not join in the hue and cry. The letters
were cant. They were revoltingly pious and echoed each
other with a dreadful sameness which suggested that we had
Max Eastman's artists in uniform on our side of the fence,
too. I knew nothing at first hand about Communist-
dominated organizations, real or alleged, and I simply could
not bring myself to sit down and write two paragraphs of
hollow rhetoric which I did not really feel.

Had it not been for the success of *With Malice*, I am
sure I would have gone along with the crowd. But my experience at the time that book came out had made me think that
sometimes what is accepted by everybody as beyond question
is far from being the product of rational thought. And once
again life was force-feeding me, for I had an obligation to ful-
fill, that particular weekend of the Waldorf Conference,
which seemed to throw the anti-Communist stampede into
its proper perspective.

As the author of *Color Blind*, I had been invited to go to
an extremely prosperous town in New Jersey and speak to a
group of high school teachers who were proposing to set up a

civics course that would be attended by pupils from both the town's high schools—the white one and the one for blacks. In this community, even the children's sleigh-riding was segregated. The well-to-do people lived in the hilly part of town and the black people lived where it was flat, but when the black children took their sleds up to the steep streets, they were driven off by the coupon-clipping hillbillies.

The teachers who wanted to set up the interracial civics course had tenure, so they could not be fired, but they were being subjected to every possible kind of harassment to get them to drop the idea. The white pupils who were interested in the project were also being strongly pressured at home to leave it alone. Knowing the ruthlessness of the opposition, we all started off the meeting with pounding hearts, but it ended up as a great success. And one thing was completely absent from it. Hollow rhetoric. That little group of people, challenging so courageously in their obscure and unpublicized way an almost impregnable citadel of prejudice, rang true.

When I look back over my life, it seems to have been about equally divided between rage and happiness.

The two do not go together?

In some natures, they succeed each other like night and day.

"If American society is going the way I think it is going," I wrote in my diary in 1949, "I am not going along with it."

What arrogance! Who did I think I was, to set myself up as an arbiter of the way things ought to be? But some of the people I most admired had set themselves up as arbiters of the way things ought to be. Thoreau, for instance. Or Eleanor Roosevelt. More importantly, Joseph and I were both concerned with the way things ought to be because we had a daughter. Celia was a member of a generation. All over the country, children were growing up who would be her friends, lovers, neighbors, doctors, plumbers and fellow voters when she reached maturity, and what kind of people they were as adults would have a great deal to do with her happiness or unhappiness.

I always think of my daughter's generation as the Howdy-Doody babies, because just about the time they got old enough to look at television, a program advertising Howdy-Doody cookies was turned on every evening in almost every house in the country where there were children. It did not seem as if the Howdy-Doody babies were being groomed for a judicious maturity. In the early years of their lives, we appeared to be reaching a point where bishops would stand in front of their altars and smilingly plug Howdy-Doody communion wafers. ("They Don't Stick to the Roof of Your Mouth.")

And at the same time that more and more previously inviolate sanctuaries were being invaded by commercialism, there was an increasing drift politically toward government by what Edith Wharton once called "unpetitionable powers." Senator McCarthy did what he pleased, and the people he denounced could not sue him for libel because he made his charges on the floor of the Senate, where he was immune from libel suits. It seemed to Joseph and me that the ethical heritage of the Howdy-Doody babies was being recklessly squandered in the supposedly sacred name of "fighting Communism."

More than anything else, children need protection from paradox. You have to be mature and fully developed to be able to cope with paradox. But the decade of the 1950s, when the Howdy-Doody babies were growing up, was above all else paradoxical. Political life brimmed with savagery, but nonpolitical life was flaccid and inane. Growing children heard adults talking about Russian and American cities being "taken out" in nuclear war. The Rosenbergs were executed for espionage, though never before in peacetime had the death sentence been imposed for that crime. And many people described Vice-President Nixon, admiringly, as having "an instinct for the jugular."

But while punitiveness and vengefulness ran rampant in the political arena, the psychologists, personnel managers and human relations experts were talking sweetness and light. They coined the word "togetherness" and stressed the importance of belonging. Being able to get along with the group was postulated as the most important of all personality traits, and such a premium, in fact, was put on being colorless, inoffensive and assimilable that a man was considered bristlingly aggressive if he shook the water off his celery before eating it.

"Ah, but," the reader will object, "the foregoing is not much of a paradox, because children do not take any interest in politics and therefore cannot be influenced by them." True. But their parents are influenced by the political climate—even parents who do not bother to vote—and parents influence children. "There is no private life," George Eliot wrote in *Felix Holt*, "that is not determined by a wider public life."

As a matter of fact, "privatism" was the word used by the sociologists to describe the way in which many adults in the 1950s retreated from any responsibility for public affairs and tried to make their homes and bringing up their children the main focus of their lives. And who could blame them? They were retreating from things they did not understand and on which they could only comment by saying helplessly, "The rules are changed."

The rules were indeed being changed, and in my view, one of the major things that changed them was the two trials of Alger Hiss. Many people were disturbed by the conduct of the Hiss case and thought either that the defendant was in-

nocent or that the verdict should have been the Scottish one
of Not Proven. But they believed—or encouraged themselves
to hope—that deplorable and even shocking as it was, in the
end it would all blow over and things would go back to the
way they used to be.

I was more than disturbed by the Hiss case. I was obsessed by it. I was obsessed because I believed as passionately
as I had ever believed anything in my life that things were
not going to return to the way they used to be. I wanted to
stand on the rooftops and scream to the assembled multitude,
"WE ARE TAKING THE WRONG TURNING!" Like a
great many other people, I made a strong personal identification with the defendant—perhaps, in my case, because he
evoked memories of Mrs. Loeffler. But I was not thus deeply
aroused because of a noble and generous impulse to cham-
pion a beleaguered hero. My reaction was a selfish one. I
wanted me and mine to be safe, and I was convinced that a
climate of fear was being created which would not disappear
when the final verdict was in and in which I and mine would
feel anything but safe.

The Hiss case went on seemingly forever and I agonized
over every setback suffered by the defense. But, as often happened in situations where I was all stirred up emotionally,
there was a comic aspect; and the comic aspect in this instance was that I was hoist on my own petard. I had been
self-congratulatory about Joseph's and my wanting to live a
three-dimensional life and have a certain prescience about
the future, but had not considered that intuition might sketch
out a future which it would be more comfortable not to
foresee. Cassandra, too, had had a certain prescience about
the future, and Cassandra was not an odds-on favorite for the
Woman of the Year Award in 1200 B.C.

Alger Hiss certainly invited some of the punishment he
got. He did not help himself, at the beginning of the first

trial, by correcting the pronunciation of the government's lawyers. But it seemed to me, and to others, outrageous that anyone should be detained in court for as much as five minutes on the evidence of Whittaker Chambers, the penitent ex-Communist who denounced Hiss.

It happened that I had once worked briefly for Chambers when he was Book Editor of *Time*. At one point it was suggested that my writer's block which followed upon the publication of *With Malice* might get unstuck if I had a regular, not-too-taxing writing assignment. Strings were pulled and I got the job of doing the short book reviews in *Time* that came at the end of the long review. The task proved to be of no help in getting me back to writing and I gave it up after a few months. Chambers I found to be unbelievably and inexplicably churlish, and when I reported this in great distress to Henry, he said the man was no doubt envious of the success of *With Malice*, which he probably considered entirely undeserved.

When Chambers blazed into the headlines some years after my fleeting contact with him, he revealed himself in his testimony as so slippery a character that he made the average eel seem fossilized. But though he was a self-confessed perjuror with a very dubious past, *The Saturday Evening Post* changed its cover format for the first time in a hundred years in order to give appropriate emphasis to the serialization of his book, *Witness*.

Most journalists who wrote about Chambers described him as an enigma. It seemed to me, however, that they were too ready to take him at his own valuation. My belief was that Whittaker Chambers at heart did not give a solitary damn about saving the country from Communism. What motivated him was that he was disreputable and socially unacceptable, and the thing he was really after was respectability. But it was respectability *as it is conceived of by some-*

body who has never had any. His upbringing had been weird, to say the least, so he did not know that respectability means things like your word being as good as your bond.

There is still a coterie of American intellectuals who also knew Chambers personally and to whom, to this day, he seems like a witness to whom a defendant's reputation and personal liberty could be safely entrusted. And one can well see why, because Chambers's intellectual attainments were dazzling. He taught me in ten minutes how to write *Time*-style, and I am no chameleon when it comes to altering my habitual mode of expression. But it is possible to have an exceptionally fine mind and still be in essence a primitive.

There are certain Stone Age tribes who believe that if you kill your brave enemy and eat his heart, you acquire his courage. My hunch was that Whittaker Chambers thought that respectability could be acquired that way, too. If he "killed" Alger Hiss, he would magically acquire the Hiss respectability and it would not matter how many times he had reversed his sworn testimony.

My first Lame Duck had been a pathological liar. His native intelligence was first-rate. He could not otherwise have held down the job he had for as long as he did. But he was a severely damaged character who could not stand the impingement of reality. When reality got too close to him, he simply said, not what was true, but what he wished had been true. And when he was caught flat out in a lie, he was not even faintly or momentarily embarrassed. He just laughed and said, "Oh, *that.* . . ."

But my first Lame Duck was a private person who had harmed nobody but himself. In Whittaker Chambers, on the other hand, a pathological liar was—it seemed to me—being structured into the culture as a responsible man and a reliable witness. And an ominous feeling grew on me, as the trials progressed, that Chambers was being structured into the culture—not in spite of the fact that he was a liar but *because* he was a liar. The implications for the future, if that were true, were horrendous.

But of that, more later.

In 1951, Reinhold died.

I had been aware, in the last seven years of my father's life, that he and I could never make up for what we might have had if things had been different. It had to be a truncated relationship. Nevertheless, ever since the day of Joseph's remark on the bus, we had had a kind of tacit friendship—a mutual respect—which I think meant as much to him as it did to me. We did not talk about my books. He had the self-educated man's fear of discussing anything literary with a person who had been to college, and I did not try to drag him beyond what he considered his depth. But he knew, through what I had written, something of what I was like.

Though it showed only in the look in his eyes when the future was mentioned, he was afraid of dying, and I was helpless to do anything more than perform little services for him, to show he had my attention, and sometimes to put a hand on his shoulder. But in the event, my last recollection of him was one of dauntlessness and mischief. He died of arteriosclerosis, and toward the end, though he was conscious, his mind wandered and he did not recognize people. I went into his hospital room one afternoon and said, "Hi, Pop. It's Margaret. Do you know me?"

He gave me a bright glance. "No," he said, "but I'd like to buy you a beer."

Joseph was a tower of strength, when the end came, and the comfort he was able to offer was balm in Gilead, but the aching sense of loss haunted me for a long time. This was partly because I had not been able to share my feelings with my mother and sister. I am sure that, in their respective

ways, they felt Reinhold's passing, but anything more than a
decorous solemnity at the funeral would have seemed to
them like emotional self-indulgence.

Reinhold's death was not the only milestone which occurred (if milestones can be said to occur) at that time. The
year before, Joseph and I had taken the last of the money
from *With Malice* and bought a house in Westchester
County, New York, so that Celia would have fresh air and
green grass and a place in which to play. We lived in that
house for sixteen years, and we were very happy in it. It was a
small, imitation-Tudor dwelling on a rather cramped piece of
ground, but it had an open fireplace which we used all
winter and a stone-flagged, tree-shaded screened porch on
which we practically lived in the summertime.

We made good friends in Westchester—how good was
to be demonstrated sometime later. We attended the Unitarian church, and for two years in a row I was cookie chairman of Celia's Brownie troop. At home, I made curtains and
bedspreads, painted the kitchen and bathroom, planted
bulbs, mowed the lawn and had people to dinner. The care
of the house, both inside and out, was very much my prov-
ince. Joseph was willing to be helpful, but he was a manual
defective. He could unbend a paper clip so that it was in a
straight line, but for any task involving the maintenance of
real property, he seemed to have been born with mittens on
his hands.

However, he was a wonderful father to Celia, and it was
to him that I owed the satisfying and stabilizing reconcili-
ation with Reinhold. Also, he cared a great deal about my
writing. An inspired and untiring editor, he saved me from
making awful *gaffes* and with judicious praise reanimated me
when the will-to-do flagged and sank to the ground. I was
also unendingly impressed by his wealth of information. It
did not matter what oddment of knowledge you were in quest

of—a line of poetry, the date of a battle or the freight car loadings from Odessa in the summer of 1913—he always seemed to have it at the tip of his tongue. Someone has said that it is impossible to be unhappy when you are feeling grateful, and gratitude played a very large part in my half of the marriage.

Of course, we had fights. He was reduced to utter exasperation when he tried to explain the insurance policies to me and met with blank—not to say prideful—incomprehension. And I used to blow my top because he expected me to be the disciplinarian who protected our daughter's health and taught her good manners, while he curried favor with her by never denying her anything. But when I thought of the artificial tranquillity of my first marriage, compared to the experience-tested harmony of this one, it seemed like the difference between a piece of peanut brittle and a full-course meal.

Rage and happiness.

It is hard to make it sound as if I experienced them in equal proportions, although I did, because writing about rage is so much easier than writing about happiness. But the mention of rage leads back, by the most natural of transitions, to the unfinished business about the Hiss case.

I was full of fear and fury about the Hiss case while it was going on, but it seems now to have been dwarfed by the things that followed: McCarthyism, the assassination of the two Kennedys and Martin Luther King, Vietnam and Watergate. However, the turning points of history have a way of passing unnoticed at the time, and it is not unreasonable to suggest that the way in which the Hiss trials were conducted had a great deal to do with the shape of subsequent events and still has a great deal to do with the conditions under which we live today.

Three painful, alien and disorienting elements were established in the body politic at that time and they are still making themselves felt. These distorting elements were the lawless enforcement of the law, selective morality, and the one-trait personality.

"The lawless enforcement of the law" was the phrase used by a courageous (conservative) judge to describe the violence which had to be done to the statute of limitations in order to bring Alger Hiss into court at all. It was agreed by everyone that although Hiss was tried and convicted for perjury, the real charge against him was treason—the alleged passing on to Chambers of State Department papers for transmission to the Russians. But this presumed act had occurred in 1937, and by 1948 it was outlawed by the statute of limitations.

The reasoning behind the statute of limitations is that the more time that passes after a supposed crime has been committed, the harder it becomes for the accused to prove his innocence. Witnesses die or move away. Documents are destroyed or get lost. Therefore, the statute of limitations says that after a certain number of years—seven in the case of treason—a person can no longer be charged with the supposed crime.

However, there is a way to flout the clear intent of this law. Suppose you want to prove that a man committed a robbery ten years ago, but you can no longer legally bring him into court. You get him before a grand jury, put him under oath, and ask him whether he did in fact rob somebody ten years ago. If he says Yes, you cannot do anything further to him, but he stands convicted by his own admission of being a criminal. If he says No, you can charge him with perjury and, possibly, send him to jail.

People everywhere took sides in the Hiss case and disputed whether or not the defendant was guilty, but nobody took up the point which had been made by that courageous judge—i.e., that no such trials should ever have taken place. To young people today, Hiss is only a vague name, but they are familiar with the lawless enforcement of the law. They have seen it in many instances, from the use of cattle prods on black demonstrators to the murder of the four students at Kent State. And the lawless enforcement of the law first gained wide general acceptance as an allowable way of doing things with the indictment of Alger Hiss.

The second distorting element which was given official sanction by the Hiss case was selective morality. It is selective morality when white men are punished for murdering other white men, but allowed to go scot free when they murder blacks. Morality, however—and this is not theology, but plain common sense—must be unselective if it is to be enough of a force in human affairs to keep things reasonably stable. In a society which moves on wheels, everybody must stop for the red lights.

To be sure, we are all of us guilty on occasion of selective morality. Perhaps we punish one of our children for something that we let his brother or sister get away with. We call for the maximum punishment of some transgression committed by a stranger, but if the same transgression is committed by a friend, we think he should get off lightly. That is quite different, however, from setting up selective morality as official government policy, which is what was done in the Hiss case.

Chambers on his own say-so was guilty of perjury on several more occasions than the two alleged instances for which Hiss was sent to jail. However, he not only did not go to prison, but he was in his day widely acclaimed for having presumably helped to save his country from the so-called Communist conspiracy. Justice is never perfect, but its failures are usually known only to the few people involved. The Hiss case, however, was in the forefront of the public consciousness for two years before a conviction was finally obtained.

Of course, we have had other judicial *causes célèbres:* Tom Mooney and Sacco and Vanzetti. But none of the prosecution witnesses in these cases made a quarter of a million dollars, as Chambers was said to have done, out of his career on the stand. The selective morality in the government's treatment of Chambers and Hiss constituted an unmistakable social directive. That directive said, "It's all right to lie, if you are uncovering Communists in Franklin Roosevelt's State Department."

Somewhere along the way, however, the conditional clause got lost and the abbreviated directive became simply, "It's all right to lie." This was a marvelously convenient sanction for a society accustomed to spending ten billion dollars a year on advertising. People in the 1950s, remembering an earlier directive which went, "Thou shalt not bear false witness," said in bewilderment, "The rules are changed." They might with more accuracy have said, "The brakes are off." Just a few short years after the American government staged its pageant of selective morality about Hiss and Chambers, that government was itself lying about the casualties in Vietnam and the bombing of Cambodia.

The third distorting element with which we are still living today, and which was solidified by the Hiss case, is the one-trait personality. It has been a little-noted aspect of mass communications that, wishing to reach the widest possible audience, it has always presented prominent people in very simple terms. Famous people—sports stars, entertainers, political figures—were clearly labeled for the convenience of the public, and the label usually consisted of only one word. Thus Dwight Eisenhower was genial, Bing Crosby was relaxed, Adlai Stevenson was indecisive, Marilyn Monroe was sexy and John F. Kennedy was young.

Whittaker Chambers and Alger Hiss would have lived and died unknown, but for the institution of the one-trait personality. Never mind that a great many people reacted to Mr. Chambers as to a hair on the tongue. His label was "patriot," and that made it impossible to send him to jail. And it made the other protagonist, *ipso facto*, a traitor.

The one-trait personality was in the making before the Hiss case, but the Hiss trials helped materially to establish it in the minds of many people as a true picture of reality. The victims of the McCarthy inquisition which followed upon the heels of the Hiss case were often people who had devoted themselves to socially constructive goals. Nevertheless, when they were hauled up before McCarthy's Permanent Investigations Subcommittee, the respect and esteem they had earned, sometimes over most of a lifetime, counted for nothing. Their solitary characteristic was that they were betrayers, and they were treated accordingly.

Not willingly does a writer, even a come-to-Jesus one like the undersigned, broach a topic like the Hiss case which older people would like to forget and young people have barely heard of. But it is possible to argue that the way in which the Hiss trials were conducted brought into American life something which had not been there before and which has since come to be a dominating feature of American society—to wit, the institutionalized lie. In Lyndon Johnson's administration it was called a credibility gap, but the original credibility gap—the prototype, the pilot project—was in Whittaker Chambers's testimony. And the final official sanction of the institutionalized lie came when all the sordid perjurings and palpable falsehoods of Watergate ended with President Ford pardoning Richard Nixon.

For some years after my Lame Duck period, I cringed to recall it—blushing to think I had been such a fool. But when enough time had passed to soften the recollection, I came eventually to understand why my second Lame Duck had risked the displeasure of a generous benefactress by secretly getting married. The whole setup had been too rich for his blood. It would have been too rich for anybody's. The lesson to be learned was that generosity is not enough. One must also have the intelligence not to give the recipients of one's bounty more than they have the capacity to receive.

Later on, when Joseph and I were bringing our daughter up in Westchester, this lesson came in handy. There seemed to be a child psychologist on every street corner in our community, and the one indictment we mothers and fathers came to dread was having our children called "insecure." But how could you make the children feel secure when you felt insecure yourself because the rules were changed?

> Man was made for joy and woe,
> And if this we truly know,
> Safely through the world we go.

That was William Blake's idea of security, but the overruling criterion by which middle-class parents were judged, and by which they judged themselves, was whether the children were happy. In a desperate attempt to keep them happy, the parents made the same mistake I had made with my second Lame Duck. They gave the rising generation more than it was able to accept—more indulgence, more advantages, more playthings. Once when Joseph and I were going over my diaries, he had said to me, "The bad thing about your childhood was that you had responsibility without authority." Now, so many years later, that situation seemed to have been stood on its head. The Howdy-Doody babies had authority without responsibility.

This mistaken policy was just as hard on the older generation as it was on their offspring. One of my neighbors, a woman who had a prosperous husband and four children, summed up in a single sentence what it was like to be a Howdy-Doody parent.

"I'm lonely," she said, "and there aren't enough letters in the local paper saying I'm a good mother."

At that point I realized that my mind had been shaping up for quite a while to write another book.

Supposedly, the remedy for people's loneliness and feeling of not being appreciated was immediately at hand, and that remedy was, of course, consumerism. Today there are hippies and dropouts abundantly in evidence, their operatic tatterdemalion making a conscious mockery of acquisitiveness. Twenty years ago, however, the people of college age were so little disposed to protest that they were called the Silent Generation, and nobody dreamed that there would ever be such a thing as a counterculture.

Both Joseph and I had been brought up frugally, but we were certainly not strong enough to stand austerely aside, immune to the ceaseless pressure to buy, use up, throw away and buy again. We were both of us depressed and disgusted by the exclusive emphasis on material possessions, and we stopped taking the Sunday papers because they were so obscenely swollen with advertising. Nevertheless, we got sucked in, just like everybody else. We found ourselves saying things like "This room would look better with a . . ." or "We could save a lot of money if we had . . ." Much has been written about the Affluent Society, but few people have tried to spell out definitively the powerful attraction it exerted. It was like living on the slopes of Venusberg. But without an exit visa.

The book I started working on—to help myself resist the pressures of consumerism—was called *The Folks at Home*

and I hoped it would prove to be an exit visa from Venusberg. Since spending was what we were supposed to do to the
limit of our capacity, why not do it with awareness instead of
mindlessly? If one examined the nature of spending, the book
suggested, there seemed to be three kinds. The first was what
might be called protoplasmic spending—the money laid out
for food and shelter. Then there was defensive spending—the
things bought because everybody else was buying them and
because not to buy them would give one the name of an eccentric. The third kind of spending was escape spending.
This was money used to give one a momentary sense of
power, and that sense of power was like the enhancement an
alcoholic feels from taking the first drink of the day. The
basic flaw in mindless spending—though at that time it was
flatteringly referred to as "the good life"—was that it was
lonely.

But *The Folks at Home* was principally concerned with
the contradictions that made bringing up children at that particular juncture so far from being the rewarding responsibility
it should have been. The contradictions had always been
there. There had been the Judeo-Christian ethic which said,
"Lay not up treasures for yourself upon earth," and there had
been the robber barons. Time passes, however, and things
change. The robber barons had paid no heed to the Gross
National Product and had tolerated the Judeo-Christian ethic
provided it stayed somewhere out in left field. But in our day
the G.N.P. was an overriding consideration and the Judeo-
Christian ethic, it seemed to me, was under direct attack—
though the attack was carefully disguised.

> The American business society [so ran the conclusion
> of the book] is currently self-hypnotized. It has persuaded it-
> self that in celebrating the importance of money and the su-
> periority of the money-making personality, it is fighting

Communism. What the business society is actually doing is engaging in a compulsive attempt to destroy our traditional national morality. By means of an ostensible crusade against Communism, it is trying to bring into general acknowledgement and good repute a kind of behavior which will have all the appearance of being an ethic, but which will not raise any awkward questions about the money-changers in the Temple.

The Folks at Home was a long time in the making—it was not published until 1952—because I found it an inordinately difficult book to write. I was terrified that I might merely be making myself ridiculous. Might there not be some special body of knowledge to which everyone but me had access and which invalidated all my thinking? And the society, careering like a runaway horse toward an ever greater affluence, seemed unstoppable. When I thought of what I was trying to say, and the national climate in which I was proposing to say it, my heart failed me.

The foregoing is a plea offered in extenuation, because I was not easy to live with while *The Folks at Home* was in the works. I did not want life to pass me by without trying in some tiny way to grapple with the problems of my time. Commendable enough. But the sinking feeling which practically never left me—the tight, hard, unassuageable apprehension—made me frequently arbitrary, demanding and a snapper-out of commands; and when I was not being dictatorial, I was being dejected.

I was also quiveringly defensive, and Lee Wright, my editor at Simon and Schuster, got used to my exiting in high dudgeon because of some criticism she had made, only to creep back later and admit shamefacedly that she had been right. She, however, never wavered in her encouragement. Nor did Joseph. When I worried about the amount of Scotch it required for me to be able to get to sleep at night, Joseph quoted Richard Hughes, author of *High Wind in Jamaica*, who had said that writing creates tensions which can only be relaxed by drink or travel.

But when the book was finally delivered to the publishers, the man who was in charge of sales and promotion called up and said that, in his view, this was the best manuscript which had ever come into the house. We were just finishing dinner when the call came, and when in a transport of excitement I returned to the dining room to report on it, Joseph grinned all over his face and said, "*Nu*, Mrs. Great Writer, do I have to do the dishes alone?"

Unfortunately, the fellow at Simon and Schuster turned out to be the one swallow who does not make a summer. When *The Folks at Home* was published, it dropped like a plummet into an abyss of silence. It was not reviewed in any of the important places, and the very few critics who took note of it wrote with such gingerliness that a reader of the review could not have told what the book was about.

I reeled with the shock. I had grown up enough since the publication of my second book to expect that with this one, shots would be fired, not across my bows, but smack into them. But I had hoped that the book would start a little discussion, and had assumed that because of the success of *Color Blind*, there would be at least a minimal acknowledgment of my existence. The no-person treatment caught me completely off balance. How could you steer for the sound of the guns when there were no guns?

A long time later, I could see that some of the ideas put forward in *The Folks at Home* were the same ideas that underlay the alternative society, but in 1952, things had not yet gotten bad enough for that kind of thinking to evoke any response. At the time, however, I had no such consoling perspective and felt scaldingly humiliated. I had given my little all, and the mandarins who determine the fate of published books had turned away with a polite vomiting motion. I was still unshakably convinced that there were people who reacted as I did to the way middle-class life was shaping up, but it seemed as if I could only reach them by standing around barefoot on the pavement, dressed in a burlap robe with a rope around the waist and handing out tracts to passersby.

"Night and silence. Who is here?"

Confronted with such a rejection, what was the happy Protestant—the self-appointed guide to the Good, the True, and the Beautiful—going to do next? That was the problem.

7
Steady the Buffs

The first thing was to work my fingers to the bone for Adlai Stevenson.

Oh, the fragrance of that name!

One of Stevenson's biographers who greatly admires him says that the Governor was sometimes selfish and inconsiderate in his personal relationships; and toward the end of his career, he disappointed many of his still-loyal adherents by not resigning as U.S. Ambassador to the U.N. when it turned out he had been lied to about Cuba. But to those Americans who, way back in 1952, were dismayed by the rising tide of mediocrity, the emergence of Adlai Stevenson as a national political figure was like the coming of a Redeemer. It was not just the grace and wit and charm, or even, on a more practical level, Stevenson's excellent record as Governor of Illinois. It was that he said, "Let's talk sense to the American people." The hungry sheep looked up and glimpsed the possibility of a square meal.

Working for Stevenson was an experience in which joy, hope and excitement were mingled with the keenest apprehension, for the Stevenson volunteers encountered an infuriating phenomenon. It was to be anticipated that the press would come out almost *en bloc* on the Republican side. They always had. But people one might have expected to plump for the Democratic candidate nevertheless did not. *The Nation*, for instance, supported Eisenhower, and Walter Lippmann said that while Stevenson was clearly the better man and would make the better President, the Republicans had been out of power for so long that if they did not win this time around, they were likely to turn Fascist.

"Mr. Lippmann," I said to my fellow workers, "is reading Stevenson out of the White House with bell, book and candy."

I was in despair when my candidate lost to Eisenhower, because it seemed to me that the voters had made a frivolous choice, and that when you have made one frivolous choice, it gets easier and easier to make more of them. Stevenson's defeat, in fact—coming after the silence that had greeted *The Folks at Home*—proved to be too much for my psychic equipment. The death of Reinhold the preceding year may have been a factor, too. At any rate, I had a nervous breakdown. It did not arrive, as had the phobia, between one second and the next. It unfolded petal by petal, like one of Baudelaire's Flowers of Evil.

Even now it is painful to read the entries in my diary at that time. Panic comes up from the pages like steam from a plate of soup, but it is displaced onto all kinds of unsuitable objects. I was beside myself with worry about money, although it was not necessary. True, *The Folks at Home* had not brought in the income we had hoped for, but Joseph was steadily getting salary increases and we were not committed to big monthly payments for installment buying. (This was due to my influence. Joseph was by now far from being the improvident Bohemian of his salad days, but he still had extravagant impulses which he permitted me to curb.)

It is clear in the diary, however, that I was thinking of

the financial disappointment about the book in a way completely divorced from reality. Indeed, I sometimes drove over to the poorest part of town and with tears running down my cheeks, sat and looked at the local tenements—in one of which, I was convinced, we would soon be living. But the worst encroachment of dementia was that the phobic terror—in what I regarded as the greatest sellout of all time—began very rapidly to invade the house, so that there were mornings when I was so afraid to leave the bedroom and go downstairs to fix breakfast that I descended hand over hand on the banisters, like a person out of bed for the first time after a long illness.

Fortunately, some days were better than others, or I could not have survived the battering I was taking, and nowhere in the diaries is there a single mention of suicide, for the idea did not cross my mind. I wept, and at the worst times begged to be sent away to a mental hospital. But this was rhetoric, as Joseph sensed—poor Joseph!—for had I been taken up on the proposition, I would have refused to go. At the very bottom level, beneath the layers and layers of *Sturm und Drang*, was a basic optimism; and a stranger reading those diaries would probably conclude my main trouble to have been that, no more than the street lamp on the corner, did I know how to ride the punches.

I tried to ride them, as the symptomology progressively developed, by having recourse to alcohol. By clinging to my sense of responsibility for Celia, I managed to get through the daytime routines, though the usual state of my sensibilities was about that of the British Expeditionary Force at Dunkirk. In the evenings, however, when Celia and Joseph had gone to bed, I sat up for hours by myself, slowly and methodically taking tiny sips of Scotch and wallowing in fantasies in which I rebuilt life so that it was more to my liking. The cartoonist Jules Feiffer once said that the one great fantasy all Americans have is getting even, and in this respect I was American to the core.

Liquor did not make me sick or affect my gait, and I never had hangovers, but the drinking did have one disastrous result. Periodically and completely unpredictably, it had the effect of releasing all the bottled-up rage beneath the surface, and on these nights I kept Joseph up until three in the morning while I ranged like a tigress over the vast landscape of my grievances. They were infinitely repetitious, those jeremiads. Even when I was scuppers awash with Johnny Walker, I still had enough vestigial sense of style to be aware that this endless chewing over of the same thing in the same phrases was as boring to the listener as seeing a B picture for the twentieth time. But the luxury of expressing rage and giving vent to fury was so seductive—so totally exquisite—that it precluded self-editing.

Every self-respecting autobiography—and this one is no exception—has intermittent, fully orchestrated crescendos about How I Suffered! But the corollary—How I Made Others Suffer (no exclamation point)—is usually rendered in the softest of pianissimos. I was faintly aware, but only faintly, that Joseph had a job to hold down while this *crise de nerfs* was going on at home and that my desperate phone calls to him during the day were a considerable handicap to his working life He was inexhaustibly patient, and Dr. Cotter, luckily, was sympathetic and helpful, but obviously something had to be done. For Celia's sake, if for no other reason. Fruitless as it had been before, there seemed no alternative but to have another go at psychoanalysis. I went to a woman practitioner who had an office in our neighborhood, and this time I struck it lucky.

Dr. J. was tall and stately and one tended to visualize her pouring tea at a table freighted with Georgian silver. But she was gentle and sensitive and—what was a bonanza for me—she seemed able to empathize with phobic terror as no one had before. I owe her a lot. I had not been going to her very long when the phobia retreated to its former boundaries outside the house. And even there, after a while, it began by infinitesimal degrees to diminish in intensity and the "abused and abusive" evenings, as Joseph and I called them, occurred less frequently.

I went to Dr. J. for two years, and I was not "cured" when I left her. But even when I was still going to her, there was enough of a loosening of binding, blinding attitudes— like the neurasthenic fears about money—for Joseph to say that the summer of 1953 was one of the happiest he had ever spent.

However, while I, to my husband's and my daughter's infinite relief, was going onward and upward toward the stars, the country was fast going in the opposite direction. Like some huge octopus, the institutionalized lie was coiling one tentacle after another around the body politic. McCarthyism was in full swing, and the United States had become a continent-wide lunatic asylum. In what was called the Little Hiss case, a brilliant young economist named William Remington, who worked for the government, was sent to jail for perjury because he had said that when he was a student at Dartmouth, fifteen years previously, he had been unaware that there was a branch of the Young Communist League on campus.

Part of the terror of the McCarthy era came from the fact that McCarthyism was continuously insulting to the intelligence and thus affected everyone in the country, whether he or she had a left-wing record or not. There was a piledriver pressure which no one could escape to accept Illogic and Unreason as normal mental processes. For instance, Communist principles and Communist practice were supposed to be loathsome to every freedom-loving American.

But at the same time these principles and this practice were by inference so compellingly attractive that anyone exposed to them, even at second or third hand, would immediately succumb to their powerful lure. Hence it was necessary for Congressional committees to "investigate" whole professions—teachers, government employees and even Hollywood entertainers.

There was an attraction involved, but it was not the attraction of Communism. Even the decentest human being, appalled as he was, could not help feeling a tiny, furtive stirring of excitement at the activities of Senator McCarthy. Whom would he attack next? How far would he go? "The good life," though it spawned comforts, was a bit dull and slander livened it up.

We had come a long way, in a very short time, from "Let's talk sense to the American people." Nevertheless, there was considerable unease about the reckless invasions of Constitutional rights and in 1954 I was asked by the League of Women Voters in our town to give a speech on civil liberties. In the speech I said that while these invasions were often justified on the grounds that we were up against an unscrupulous enemy, the real enemy was unscrupulousness itself, no matter in whom it occurred.

The speech made several other points that would seem now like mere ordinary common sense; but it was received in stunned silence, and a few nights afterward somebody came under cover of darkness and painted "Dirty Communist" and a string of obscenities on the side of our house. The local paper, to which everyone subscribed, printed the longest editorial it had ever run calling me a dupe of the Communists, and for six or seven weeks afterward its Letters column seethed with communications which hammered away at "Miss Halsey's long list of Red-front activities."

And what about that long list?

Great play was made of the fact that I had not denounced the Waldorf Conference of the I.C.C., but that was
about the only thing in it of actual substance. "Margaret Halsey?" some nameless operative in the F.B.I. said to himself.
"A writer? Obviously, writers support bookshops." And down
it went in my dossier—"Supporter of 11 Communist bookshops." The institutionalized lie.

Compared to what happened to others, I was only
brushed by the wing tip of McCarthyism. Some of the New
York City schoolteachers, when a Congressional committee
turned the spotlight in that direction, were deluged with poi-
son pen letters and scurrilous phone calls. I got only one
such phone call. A lady rang up to ask me why I didn't go
back to the synagogue where I came from—which was a
pretty fair indication of some of the soldiery that was being
mustered to protect us from the Communist menace.

Even today, however, it is heartwarming to remember
how loyally Joseph's and my friends rallied around. Their letters to the paper, generously and indignantly supporting me,
were lost in the tidal wave of communications calling me a
traitor; but their adherence made all the difference in the
world. They could not have helped being frightened, because
they were defying what was in effect a lynch mob and all
around them—both locally and nationally—people who were
supposed to have integrity were equivocating, temporizing
and playing safe.

In the last thirty years we have not been lacking in supposed heroes, from Eisenhower to Kissinger, but in my own
personal experience, it has always been obscure people who
turned out in the clinches to have genuine stature—my
friends in Westchester, the schoolteachers in that wealthy
New Jersey suburb, or Reinhold refusing to ostracize Mrs.
Loeffler during World War I.

Much more typical, for those times, than my friends'

behavior was the reaction of the Unitarian minister, who up till then I had considered a fine fellow. He telephoned me right after the local paper's editorial appeared and said in a voice reedy with fright, "Don't answer them. Just keep quiet. Just lie low." Obviously, he was in a dither of apprehension that he would be tarred with my brush because I was a member of his church.

Actually, I had already answered them with all guns blazing, but the bold stance I adopted in the public prints was quite at variance with what I felt in private. All the while the brouhaha was going on, the plop with which the newspaper landed on the front walk every evening sounded like the crack of doom and I had such a nervous stomach that I subsisted largely on apples, milk and handfuls of salted peanuts. But later on, when things had quieted down, it was borne in on me how sound is the old psychological maxim that we become what we fear. The hysterical, maniacal fear of totalitarianism was making us totalitarian, too, with the same brutal punishment for dissent and the same subservience to the Ritual Lie.

One unexpected result of the League of Women Voters speech was that it produced an estrangement between my sister and me that turned out to be permanent. My brother-in-law had been a naval lieutenant during the war and he and Mary were stationed for the duration in the South, where—perhaps inevitably—they absorbed some of the attitudes of white Southerners about black people. The stilted communication between my sister and me managed somehow to survive the publication of *Color Blind*, though she and her husband came back from the South saying "nigger"—which they would then correct, in my presence, by laughing and saying elaborately, "I beg your pardon, Knee-Grow." But in the 1950s they became ardent admirers of Senator Joseph McCarthy, and when somebody sent Mary a copy of the edi-

torial attacking me, she wrote me a furious letter saying it was
time I stopped worrying about my colored friends and paid a
little attention to my family.

I could sympathize. Mary was a schoolteacher, and that
profession was the object of particular scrutiny by the fer-
reters-out of Communism. Also, the most tenuous contacts
with others had come to be construed as guilt by association.
My sister did not ask me whether it was really true that I had
been active in Communist-dominated organizations. For
her, as for many others at that time, the mere accusation was
in itself a proof of guilt. I could have told her that I had had
no idea I was supposed to have a long list of Red-front activities until I read about it in the paper, but the tone in which
she had addressed me made explanations seem like stooping.
I never answered the letter, and the rest was silence. She did
not, in the event, get into any trouble through being my sister.

If asked to describe me, Mary would have said that I was
opinionated, stubborn, selfish and a prig and that I put principles ahead of people. (Without doing any very strenuous
recruiting, she could have found those who would have
agreed with her.) To each of us, the other was the thistle in
the tossed green salad, and it would have been a toilsome effort for us to learn to accommodate to each other. The effort
would only have been worth making if we had had memories
to share of a happy family life in Lincoln Park, and since we
had no such fund of softening recollections, it was better for
us to go our separate ways.

Despite my experience in Westchester, I took a stand for
sanity whenever I could, during those years of national mad-
ness; but at this late date it would be tedious to go into over-
much detail. In 1954, William Remington was murdered in
prison by a fellow inmate. That weekend I left Celia to the
care of Joseph and shut myself in the bedroom with a bottle

of Scotch while I wrote an article called "The Natives Are Restless Tonight" which said that we had gone beyond the permissible level of injustice. Max Ascoli published the piece in *The Reporter*, but one of his editors told me that Dr. Ascoli had walked the floor all night before deciding to risk printing it.

In 1956, Senator McCarthy died, but his era did not immediately die with him, although a lot of people thought it did. As late as 1960, a well-known lecture bureau engaged me to go on tour with a humorous speech about life in the suburbs, and just before I set out, the host organization in Rockford, Illinois, said they were canceling my engagement because "Miss Halsey is listed in public documents as pro-Communist."

I told the lecture bureau that I would not go to Rockford if they did not want me, but that Rockford must pay me just the same.

"This kind of thing has happened before," said the lecture agency. "We don't make them pay. We just get you another speaking date in the same neighborhood."

"If I don't make them pay," I said, "it looks as if I were accepting their view of me as an undesirable person."

Rockford paid. They had to, because they had signed a contract. But the lecture bureau said they would not be interested in having me for a client the following season. Of course, I could afford to make this kind of gesture, because I had a husband to support me if my income dwindled to nothing. Others were not so fortunately placed.

Some people, as we all know, seem to go out of their way to make trouble for themselves. Why did I invite unpleasantness by impugning the motives of the sales-sensitive society in *The Folks at Home* or giving what turned out to be a provocative lecture to the League of Women Voters? God knows, I could not hope to be effective. I was a field mouse squeaking in the teeth of a hurricane. Nevertheless, one did in an infinitesimal way manage to communicate, and for a writer, even the tiniest amount of communication is better than none at all. I gave the League of Women Voters speech to a women's group on Long Island who had been alerted to its reception in Westchester, and they rose to their feet in a passion of gratitude when I had finished.

Of course, there was a strong argument for keeping quiet. Celia would certainly have had a more tranquil childhood if her mother had not been such a moral positivist. My daughter got used to hearing the word "upset"—"Your mother is upset"—when I was roused to the defense of some person or principle that I thought was being abused. And I was aware that an embattled mother is not the ideal maternal type. Or, at least, was not so considered back in the days before we had Women's Lib.

On the other hand, I was also conscious of having been bequeathed an ethical heritage—directly, by Reinhold, Miss Sibley, the Boltons, Cheney and Dorothy Canfield Fisher and indirectly by others. I believed that when my daughter was grown up, she would think it was better to have had that heritage affirmed in a time of stress than to have had it sacrificed for the sake of a false calm. I was, after all, a writer and therefore in a better position than people in other callings to speak up.

And of course I was not always upset. Far from it. I remember one summer evening when Celia was about eight years old and Joseph came home from the office and said dramatically, "I got on the train at Grand Central, and when I got off here I was a different man."

He always liked to be a bit theatrical.

"In one instant," he said, "I suddenly saw that I'll have to change my attitude toward you. I've spent years holding your hand and giving you emotional support, and it suddenly came to me that you don't need it the way you used to."

"Oh!" I said.

"It came to me in a flash, just the other side of Scarsdale. If I don't accommodate to your increased independence, you'll have to revert to dependence again, to preserve the marriage. Or else you'll eventually go off and find somebody else to be married to."

"Never," I said, "but tell me more," and added fervently, "You're warming the cockles of my heart."

I felt the same euphoria I used to experience back in P.S. 21, where effort was recognized. Joseph, however, was prevented from elaborating because just at that moment Celia came running in, proclaiming that she was starved.

"Everything's ready. Go and wash your hands."

I floated into the kitchen. To realize that, after twelve years of marriage, one is being looked at with an eye unglazed by habit . . .

I suppose I remember that particular evening because of what Joseph had said upon coming home, for otherwise it was not unlike most of our evenings. French doors led out to our porch, with a window on either side, and Celia usually preferred to climb out through one of the windows. She arrived head first at her seat at the table, which was just under the window; there was a brief moment of sunburned legs describing arcs in the air; and then she righted herself.

I put a casserole down and took the lid off. She half rose to peer into it and said, "Chicken! Oi-kuh-*foy*-kuh-FOOEY!"

This was an expression she and her friends were currently using to comment on all events of an unexpected or a pleasant nature.

When I started serving, Celia said importantly, "Don't give Daddy any gravy." She looked at him with eyes of worship and added in turtledove accents, "Fatso Daddy."

"Just you hush up," I said sternly, and then continued

in a milder tone. "Your father is going to Take Steps about
his waistline. He's going to get a thinner knife to spread the
butter on his bagels."

"Thinner knife!" Our daughter flung herself back in her
seat, chortling. "Oi . . ."

"Kuh-*foy*-kuh-FOOEY!" said both parents at once.

"I almost said that to Angus today," Joseph remarked,
"when we finally got the person we want to teach the Wom-
en's Law course." Turning to Celia, he asked, "What did
you do today?"

"I dough know."

"Don't know," her father corrected. Our daughter's
speech pattern was more than a little slovenly. It jarred on
both Joseph and me, but our efforts to instill something
crisper would have been high on anybody's list of Famous
Lost Causes.

"We went downtown," I said, "and bought her a new
bathing suit. She's growing out of everything she owns.

"And," I added, in an altered tone, "we did the arithmetic drill."

Celia's teacher had asked us to drill her in addition and
subtraction over the summer. Joseph and I were very happy
about the fact that Celia showed great talent in her artwork,
but she had turned out to be as non-Euclidean as her mother
about mathematics. These arithmetic drills almost always
ended with Celia in tears and the presiding parent stalking
away with flared nostrils from what usually proved to be a
sort of educational Valley Forge.

Arithmetic not being a subject on which Celia cared to
dwell, she changed the subject. "Sing 'A nice girl, a proper
girl, but one of the roving kind,' " she commanded her father.

One of Joseph's great assets as a parent was that he had a

sweet, true tenor and a large repertoire of melodies old and
new.

"It's not good manners to sing at the table. Besides, I'm
eating. Your mother has surpassed herself.

"Once again," he added.

Celia held out her plate. "May I have some more,
please?" she asked politely.

Celia had been very cooperative about learning the
amenities—saying "please" and "thank you" and even writing
acknowledgments of Christmas presents with a minimum of
protest. Her father and I told each other that it was an objective truth, and not just the tunnel vision of single-child
parents, that for her age she had a certain amount of charm
and ease in social situations.

I took her plate. "A pleasure, Lady Agatha," I said.

It was an old Noel Coward line, and Celia always took it
as a personal compliment.

"Mommy said something funny this after," she told her
father. It was her habit at that time to drop the final syllable
from the word "afternoon."

Joseph looked at me inquiringly over his glasses.

"I was sorting the laundry, and I said I wished I had a
woman friend with only one ear and one foot, so I could give
her all the earrings and socks to which I had lost the mate."

Glancing through the window into the house, I saw the
laundry stacked up in neat piles on the dining room table and
said to Celia, "Before you go to bed, will you be so kind as to
take that stuff upstairs?"

How close beneath the surface dissension lies, even in
the best-regulated families! It was a bone of contention between my daughter and me that she regarded any request that
she should help around the house as a form of peonage. I for
my part thought that my emptying the garbage and sweeping

the front walk while an able-bodied child lounged on the porch swing was equally a form of peonage.

The face of the able-bodied child hardened ominously. "Why? It's perfectly all right where it is."

"I want to work on that table in the morning."

"C'n work on the porch."

"Too windy. The pages blow all over."

Celia addressed her father. "Everybody around here," she said furiously, "has to do what *she* wants, just because she's a writer."

Joseph laughed. "The last baby-sitter we had told us that the minute the door closed behind us, you took her by the hand and led her to the bookcase to show her Mommy's books."

A prideful smirk started to form itself on Celia's countenance, but then she visibly decided that this was not the stuff to give the troops. "Rotten old books," she said, but there was a hint of complacence in the tone. "Too grown-uppy."

A few children had started to gather on the lawn across the street and were sitting, standing and lying about in attitudes that seemed to suggest languid speculation about what they should do next.

One of the children called to Celia.

"May I be excused?" she said, and like Pontius Pilate, did not stay for an answer.

Her father and I watched her streak across the street and then fall instantly into the prevailing posture of contemplative idleness. We looked at each other in a flawless concord of tenderness and pride.

"She was really in a hurry," her father said. "She went out through the door."

When it comes to American politics, I am neither a Democrat nor a Republican. I am an Early Disliker, and one of the major targets of my early dislike was Dwight Eisenhower. It may seem at first blush utterly pointless—in view of all the horrors that surround us today—to revive that genial ghost. However, it is agreed by everyone that Americans today are in a state of great mental confusion and perhaps one source of that confusion may be that so far nobody has posed the question of what, exactly, constitutes a decent human being.

Eisenhower was supposed to be, whatever his failings, the very incarnation of the decent man and later on Gerald Ford enjoyed an exactly similar esteem. But why were these decent Presidents so singularly unable to impose their decency on those about them or on the events of their respective administrations? Why has their decency existed so peculiarly in a vacuum? Eisenhower's decency did not stop his closest administrative aide, Sherman Adams, from influence-peddling.

A person may be totally unimaginative and have the social vision of a mole, and we still call him a decent man, as we do Robert Carne in Winifred Holtby's *South Riding*. But he has got to have a cutting-off point—a place where he draws the line. And this basic essential of decency, Eisenhower lacked. Not that he was a scoundrel. He was simply a paramecium—a one-celled animal that flowed around whatever foreign body happened to be in his path. It has not been generally remarked upon, but if Eisenhower had dropped Richard Nixon from the ticket when, in the Presidential campaign of 1952, it was discovered that Nixon had taken $18,000 from a group of California businessmen, Watergate could never have happened.

Early in his political career, Mr. Eisenhower had a chance to affirm a standard of decency in a way that could not have helped but attract general notice. In World War II, General George Marshall had promoted him over the heads of many others to command the European theater. Hence, when Senator Joseph McCarthy called Marshall part of a blackly traitorous plot to "lose" China, the most rudimentary good behavior required that Eisenhower should administer a stinging rebuke. But he said nothing.

His popularity with the voters was greater than anything that had ever been seen before and was always referred to in the press as "the Eisenhower magic." That so-called magic seemed to me sorely in need of anatomizing, and in 1956, after Ike's reelection, I used the occasion of the Inaugural Ball to write a piece called "A Sound of Revelry by Night."

Eisenhower's hold on the electorate was often explained by saying that he was a father image, but "Revelry" advanced the theory that what made him so unbeatable at the polls was not that he was a father image, but that he was a mirror image. He himself was the perfect prototype of the American Consumer. It was themselves that many of those voters were endorsing—their own confusion, superficiality, amorphous good intentions and evasiveness of responsibility magnified as on a huge screen in the personality of the President.

Eisenhower's inability to stand up for a friend and his unwillingness to arouse the hostility of a foe were qualities he and the shallow-rooted Consumer had very much in common. What they also had in common was a considerable anxiety to have these deficiencies interpreted, not as deficiencies, but as the ingredients of winsomeness and charm. The Eisenhower magic, therefore, was merely the President and the Consumer facing each other and saying, "Whew! For a minute there, I was scared. But if you're here, I must be real."

Naturally, in the then climate of opinion, no weekly or monthly magazine was going to touch a polemic like "Revelry" with a barge pole, and the piece ultimately appeared in the quarterly *Dissent*. But far from the madding crowd

though quarterlies are, Adlai Stevenson saw the article and
wrote me a letter saying it was the best analysis of the recent
campaign he had seen anywhere.

The whole decade of the 1950s, however, was a thin
time for the writer of polemic. Or of satire, or of anything
that had any bite to it. Despite the decent man in the White
House, it was a decade characterized by one sensational reve-
lation after another of pre-Watergate corruption. Basketball
players were discovered to have been bribed to lose games.
Disk jockeys admitted to having accepted payola. Television
quiz shows were revealed to have been rigged. White-collar
employees were found to be shamelessly stealing from their
corporate employers.

The Man in the Street, however, was not roused to in-
dignation. In fact, a standard response to these various scandals was to roll the eyes to heaven and ask piously, "Who am
I to say what's right or wrong?" The generous tolerance that
had been so stringently denied to political dissenters was,
ironically enough, available in abundance to anyone who
had been caught with his hand in the till.

Everything in the Eisenhower Era was—at least, to a
writer of tub-thumping proclivities—maddeningly soft-focus.
Novelists wrote books about the anti-hero in which a treacly
"compassion" was lavished on unsavory characters like maple
syrup poured over iron pancakes. Madison Avenue very
neatly fielded the charge of inciting to materialism by invent-
ing the phrase "people's capitalism," and some of the intellectuals, while they laughed at Eisenhower's syntax, began to
talk benignly about "the new conservatism"—which was
shorthand for "We want swimming pools, too."

Not that criticism of the American Way of Life was
frowned upon. On the contrary, it was encouraged. William
H. Whyte's *The Organization Man*, published in 1956, was
so popular that the title became a household word, and

writers of the Vance Packard school got a generous public embrace. But criticism of things American had to be of a certain kind. It had to contain, in the end, the note of resignation. When all the disturbing statistics had been quoted and all the shocking examples adduced, the final subliminal message had to be, "But we must accept these things, because they cannot be changed." Critics who believed, with Disraeli, that "Man is not the creature of circumstances; circumstances are the creature of man," were distinctly out of fashion.

In that climate of the bland leading the bland—in Arthur Schlesinger, Jr.'s, famous phrase—it was difficult to write. At least, I found it so. And there is a note in my diary for 1954 that Joseph threw down an armful of "class" magazines he had been reading and said disgustedly, "There's absolutely no thinking going on in this country at all!" For my own part—listening to or reading the received opinion of the day—I felt as if a pad soaked in chloroform were being held just a few inches away from my brain.

There was, too, the loneliness—the sense of isolation—the painful awareness that the things one wanted urgently to say were what nobody wanted to hear. Or, at least, what few people were going to be permitted to hear. There were other Early Dislikers around. In a country with America's literary and political traditions, there had to be. But when some nonconformist idea had been doggedly gotten down on paper, no journal with any substantial circulation felt able to play host to it. One intellectual fad succeeded another, and you had to write within the fads or you could not get anything into print.

I did some articles which took an unconscionable time to produce, but could only place them in magazines like The Progressive or The New Republic. Indeed, but for The New Republic, I would have been completely silenced. "It's brilliant, Miss Halsey," the other editors used to say, "but it's not for us."

As Adlai Stevenson remarked after the Presidential campaign of 1956, it was like trying to kick holes in a fog. I longed, as the hart panteth after the water brooks, for recognition, and was fiercely envious—oh, how fiercely envious!—of those tepid (for such they seemed to me) writers who commanded large audiences and were listened to respectfully.

Nevertheless, I did not regret the direction I had chosen with the writing of *Color Blind*. Of course, when you have started out with a success like *With Malice*, the childish part of your mind goes on hoping for many years thereafter that it will happen again. But the adult part (which once in a while gained ascendancy) was aware that—though I had come about as far as you could get from being the Pride of the Fifth Ward, the People's Choice—I was at least nobody's thrall.

Fortunately, what life takes away with one hand it sometimes compensates for with the other; and although my wicked fangs were clashing emptily on air, 1956 was nevertheless an *annus mirabilis* for me. In that year I finally, after more than a decade, got over the agoraphobia. The abject terror against which I had had to clench the teeth, stiffen the knees and violate the deepest instinct for self-preservation had gradually given way to a mere skittish apprehension. At least, in very familiar places around suburbia.

And then came the never-to-be-forgotten day when I turned up at Joseph's office in New York, having reached there by train and taxi—alone. The tears came to Joseph's eyes when I told him that I had made the trip by myself.

"You're a wonderful woman," he said.

At the March on Washington where Martin Luther King gave his famous I-have-a-dream speech, Lena Horne was also one of the speakers. But when she stood up and addressed the multitude, she said only one word: "Freedom."

I had not been put into a ghetto through the instrumentality of others. I had, with the phobia, involuntarily ghettoized myself.

And now the walls were down.

I did not know why I had gotten the phobia in the first place, nor why it eventually went away, but in some fashion that could not be traced, its disappearance represented growth. And one's personal growth cannot help but have a benevolent effect on those around one. For our little household, there had gradually come about a merciful lessening of intensity, for the materfamilias could now go to the bank and take the clothes to the cleaner without being brought back on her shield. In an intimate situation, one can have a little too much of Mother Courage.

For me, the sense of release which followed upon the abatement of the phobia was exquisite. No longer the stratagems to keep people from finding out. No longer the awareness that I was considered a little peculiar because Joseph turned up with me in so many places where women were not normally accompanied by their husbands. (Joseph, of course, now had a lot more free time than he had had before.) No longer going through the supermarket so blind with terror that I could scarcely read the labels on the products, surreptitiously clutching the edges of the shelves to keep from collapsing and tottering from the meats to the vegetables saying to myself, "I have a little girl to take care of . . . I must keep going because I have a little girl to take care of. . . ."

I still could not bring myself to go into the subway, but above ground I was my own mistress again. I could walk confidently, breathe freely and look boldly about me at the streets and the buildings and the people. Reality—that many-splendored thing—had reasserted itself and there was an end to cringing. This was happiness far purer and more unalloyed than anything I had experienced at the success of the first book, because it was an internal rather than an external triumph. It did not depend on good luck, or on anything done or not done by others. It could not be taken away from me. It could not lose its luster.

Triumphs, like griefs, often do not come singly, and the final, long-delayed escape from phobic terror was not the only thing that made 1956 a year of liberation in my particular calendar. In 1954 my sister and I had ceased to communicate with each other, and in 1956 the relationship between me and my mother came to an end, and in the same way—via the unanswered letter. Estrangement, it would seem, was the *specialité de la maison* in our family. The fact was, the Halseys had only been held together by the strength of Reinhold's personality, and when he was gone, the family inevitably fell apart.

But not right away. After Reinhold died, I went regularly up to Newtown to visit my mother—persuaded that it was my duty to her as my father's widow. Every visit, however, shattered me emotionally and drove me to drink when I got home. Reinhold had left his wife a modest competence and she had a new role to play. No longer the Lady Prioress, she was now the secular and worldly Rich Widow, and she was drunk with power. She exuded condescension and complacency, and made frequent references to "my investments."

Joseph saw the grotesque pathos of this stunted and distorted late-blooming, and Joseph had her right where he wanted her. One sidelong glance from him and she went down on her knees and salaamed. But me she had always been able to reduce to an idiot compliance. In 1948, when I telephoned her to tell her we were adopting a child, she was startled into silence for a moment and then she said, "Well! Don't expect *me* to do any baby-sitting for you!"

"Oh, no," I answered meekly. "Of course not," and it

did not occur to me that this was not precisely a generous response.

After Reinhold died, it became apparent that he had ridden herd on Annie to a degree one had not suspected, and her enhanced sense of herself found expression in snide, deflating remarks to me. These remarks were delivered quietly, but with an air of sparkling malice, and they had the same effect on me as rattlesnake venom. They paralyzed me. I was powerless to fight back, and either accepted them in silence or tried to turn them aside with some placating reply.

But in 1956, five years after Reinhold's death, I was finally moved to do something more constructive about my mother's denigration than just go home from Newtown and spend the whole night in a Scotch-activated rage. So, after one of our visits, I wrote her a letter protesting about something insufferable she had said. It was a hot-tempered letter— as had been the one my sister sent me about my alleged Communist sympathies—and Annie's reply was prompt and brief.

"You are an obstacle to my peace," she wrote.

Joseph leaped on it. "It's your big chance," he said. "Write and tell her that in that case, you won't inflict yourself on her any longer."

I did. She did not answer my letter, and from that day to this, I have never seen or heard from her. She is still alive. She is over ninety, and I have heard indirectly that she is in an old ladies' home, but where I do not know. Although she never baby-sat for Joseph and me, she sat all the time for my sister's three children, so she did not spend her declining years in isolation from any family context.

Was it not holding a grudge, that I never subsequently made any attempt to get in touch with her? The thought occurred to me. But there was no way I could ameliorate her basic despair, and just by walking into the same room with her, I intensified it. She was a bonnie wee Scots Gauleiter, but she was at least starkly direct. I *was* an obstacle to her peace, and it was kinder to leave her alone with her investments.

As time passed, I came to see that it had not been "strength" and a commendable sense of duty that kept me going up to Newtown after my father died. It had been mere stubbornness. I did not want to admit that I had as a child lavished all that love and devotion on an unworthy object. I was in my forties and I had a child of my own, but I never stopped hoping that some day, in some way, my mother would do or say something which showed that she loved me. She showed me instead, without intending to, something better—"the wintry smile upon the face of Truth."

8

"The Uses of the Past"

In April of 1974, when Watergate was still dominating the
news, *The New Republic* reprinted the anti-Nixon piece
which I had originally written for them sixteen years before.
The article was entitled "Beware the Tender Trap" and ran
in part as follows:

> If the Vice President's energies are truly as monumen-
> tal as the Luce publications and others in the swelling
> chorus say they are, then the Presidency in its present form
> may prove too narrow for them. Mr. Nixon, as President,
> may wish to extend the powers of his office the way those
> other dark-jowled fellows—the ones in South America—so
> often do. The opposition—the people who think that such
> an Executive should not overbalance the Legislature and
> the Judiciary—must then expect to get the "old" Nixon
> treatment. . . .
>
> Until some absolutely unmistakable portent comes
> along—such as Mr. Nixon's resigning and going to Africa as
> a missionary—common sense requires the working hypoth-
> esis that he has not changed and is not going to.
>
> To live with him as President, in full awareness of
> what his actions have shown him to be, will require consid-
> erable endurance. One's natural instinct will be to set up a

sheltering illusion—to warm up the bleak and awful truth by arguing that he cannot *really* be so bad. There will be a disposition to believe that merely sitting in an office with the American flag and the Great Seal of the United States has an ennobling effect. And so it does—but not on confirmed and habitual self-promoters.

Forced to adjust to Mr. Nixon as Chief Executive, many people will automatically develop a sort of selective morality. They will have one set of ethics—the one they were taught as children and have been used to all their lives—for judging themselves and their friends. They will have another, and a much lower one, for the President of the United States.

At first glance, this might seem like a workable compromise; but it is not. Gresham's Law operates just as immutably in ethics as it does in economics, and cheap morals tend to drive good morals out of circulation. To charitable souls, it may seem vindictive to dwell on Mr. Nixon's past, but the issue transcends considerations of charity. To remember the Vice President's record is to keep alive—if only by inversion—that standard of morality which makes life worth living. . . .

Morality is not just a picnic ground for prigs. It provides the fabric of trust which—to put it on the simplest level—enables the host to go out to the kitchen and fix drinks in the certain knowledge that his visitors will not read the letters on the desk.

When "Tender Trap" was reprinted in *The New Republic* in 1974, Harriet van Horne devoted a column to it in *The New York Post*; Henry Fairlee quoted it in an article on Watergate in the English magazine *Encounter*; Herblock used a few chunks of it in his book on Nixon, *Special Report*; and Eric Sevareid alluded to it in one of his broadcasts. In 1958, when it first appeared, the Democratic National Committee bought 300,000 copies of it for distribution to their workers.

All I got out of it was $65, but Adlai Stevenson wrote me another letter.

By 1958, however, I was growing weary of always being God's Angry Woman and wanted a change of pace, so I started work on a lighthearted book called *This Demi-Paradise: A Westchester Diary* in which Celia and Joseph and I and our various community involvements appeared under the thinnest of disguises. The book had no motivation beyond the fact that I enjoyed writing it, for I was describing things that had struck me as funny and things that had given me pleasure. There may, however, have been an additional buoyancy because in 1959, while I was still working on it, I achieved the ultimate conquest of the phobia: I rode in triumph through Persepolis on the Lexington Avenue Express.

Under the name of Cora, Celia figured largely in *This Demi-Paradise*, as did Joseph, the cats, the supermarket, the changing seasons, pollsters, liberal religion, comfortable friendships and other day-to-day experiences.

"March is the month of the Girl Scout cookie drive," ran one of the entries in the diary.

This is my second year as cookie chairman for Cora's Brownie troop and I have now learned to take it in stride. Last year, however, both the Brownies and I were new at the job, and my efforts to collate the outflow of cookies with the inflow of money bordered on the frantic.

Last year, for some reason—I suppose because the Girl Scouts wear uniforms—I was haunted by a pervasive nightmare of Prussian militarism. I could see myself being short of the required sum when the cookie drive was over. I could see the drumhead court-martial and the stern-faced women in field green. I could see the little back room where they left me with a revolver and a bottle of brandy. I could see the Girl Scout Council tapping their riding crops on the table and waiting to hear the shot which would heal the wounded honor of Troop 50, Neighborhood 6.

Actually, of course, there was not much about the enterprise to suggest the late Erich von Stroheim. On an appointed day, I waited in until some truckmen brought thirty-five cartons of cookies and left them in the middle of the living-room floor. It was a mountain of cardboard and only a supply sergeant could have thrilled to it. Then I went out to get something for dinner. When I returned, I found Cora and some friends had come in and they were playing a game for which thirty-five cartons of cookies are the well-nigh perfect equipment. The game was called Run-for-your-lives-the-dam-has-broken.

To this day, I flinch at the memory. How many people in this community bought Girl Scout cookies—expecting disks and rectangles that could be laid out neatly on a plate—and found they had purchased merely a sort of perishable gravel?

Nevertheless, the recollection comes back vividly of the day last year when Cora first wore her Brownie uniform. She stood in the hall waiting to show herself to her father—a small, cocoa-colored shape against the white banisters, her hair in pigtails to accommodate the Brownie skullcap and her face so luminous with innocent pride that it was like a candle burning in a windless place.

When her father opened the door and came in, she saluted.

Thus do the unwary fall into cookie chairmanships.

This Demi-Paradise, when it came out, did not sell so much that I was in danger of becoming a cult; but it benefited from the fact that most of the writing which was being done about the suburbs at that time concentrated on the gin-and-adultery hijinks, whereas actually many suburbanites had neither the money nor the pretensions for that kind of role-playing. A few of the reviewers were huffily dismissive because—in order to get the right degree of chiaroscuro—I had included a small McCarthyite incident which was based on an actual happening. But for the most part, the critics said that the family relationships portrayed in the book were warm and affectionate and that my humor had mellowed since the days of *With Malice*.

At that point, I should have liked nothing better than to forget about political disputation and spend the rest of my life writing little divertissements about the suburbs. It would not, however, have been possible, for middle-class life was in too much of a state of flux. Warm family relationships were getting more difficult to establish and maintain; anomie was abroad in the land; and in 1959, while I was still working on *This Demi-Paradise*, the Van Doren scandal broke.

At this late date, it seems like nitpicking even to mention the Van Doren scandal, when a television quiz show of unmatched popularity was discovered to have been rigged. But Franz Boas says that it is impossible to understand a phenomenon without going back and tracing its origins; and can there be any permanent moral rehabilitation in the United States without first having a clear comprehension of the events which contributed to the moral breakdown?

The Van Doren scandal seemed at the time to differ from the various scandals that had preceded it only because the program was estimated to have had 97 million viewers and the Van Doren family was a prestigious one. But it seemed to me the debacle fitted into a larger context, and I wrote about that larger context in a piece called "The Affluence Peddlers," which appeared in *The Progressive*.

The Affluence Peddlers were Whittaker Chambers, Dwight Eisenhower, Richard Nixon, Senator Joseph McCarthy and Charles Van Doren. These people had come boiling to the top of the social brew and enjoyed, for a shorter or a longer time, the maximum of conspicuousness.

But not through their own efforts. Not even the hard-working Mr. Nixon. Their prominence, for however long it lasted, represented the consuming society's built-in need to get rid of the puritan ethic of thrift, self-discipline and responsibility and establish instead a climate of self-indulgence.

Man is the only culture-building animal, and a society is what it is because certain people in it make significant decisions. As a result of these significant decisions, some kinds of behavior are emphasized and called to everybody's attention, while other kinds are deemphasized or even sedulously discredited. In Sparta, for instance, poets and pacifists were not given the Greek-city-state equivalent of blazing headlines and saturative publicity.

There is an old Spanish proverb which runs, "God says, 'Take what you want, and pay for it.' " What the Affluence Peddlers did, and what happened to them as a result of it, spelled out a message which was the exact opposite of the old proverb. That message was, "Take what you want. You won't have to pay for it."

Whittaker Chambers and Charles Van Doren were both perjurors, Van Doren having lied under oath before a grand jury. Neither man, however, went to prison. What Mr. Nixon and Senator McCarthy got away with scarcely needs recapitulating, and President Eisenhower, while he reveled in all the perquisites of power—the bubble-top limousine, the cheering crowds, the herd of black Angus and the cosy foregathering with millionaires—did not pay for them in the usual coin of loneliness, a hostile press and a crushing sense of responsibility.

The Van Doren scandal is significant today because it showed that what, just about that time, was beginning to be called "the new middle class" was in considerable measure not middle class at all. The real shocker about the Van Doren case was that, according to samplings of public opinion, millions of people said that Charles Van Doren had only done what they themselves would have done.

One of the hallmarks of the middle class, however—all the way back to the Reformation—had always been either actual financial probity or at least a hypocritical adherence to it in public, whatever was done in private. Hence those millions of people who refused to condemn Van Doren were anything but middle class. They were peasants—and the kind of peasants, moreover, who would have had to chin themselves to get into Balzac. The stress laid on upward social mobility in the United States has tended to obscure the fact that there can be more than one kind of mobility and more than one direction in which it can go. There can be ethical mobility as well as financial, and it can go down as well as up.

In 1960 the Kennedys came along, and a great many people with whom I usually saw eye to eye thought they stood for a young, hopeful, energetic fresh start. I would have given anything in the world to have been able to share this view, for the Kennedys made me very conscious of being a chronic sourpuss; but the hopes which rode on them seemed to me to be generated by the hunger for leadership resulting from eight years of Eisenhower and not by anything inherent in the newcomers themselves.

How likely was it that young men brought up under the close supervision of Joseph P. Kennedy, as ruthless a self-aggrandizer as ever came down the pike, were going to have liberalism and humanitarian feelings coursing through their very bloodstreams? These were not children who had rebelled against their father. On the contrary, it was a close-knit family.

To be sure, when Bobby Kennedy was killed, many competent observers noted that there was a strong mutual feeling between him and the blacks and Chicanos on the West Coast. There is no doubt this feeling was genuine on both sides. But could Bobby, as president, have maintained and developed the relationship? There are those who think so. This writer, however, is skeptical, for Bobby Kennedy's record on civil rights is chilling. He was counsel for Senator Joseph McCarthy's committee for the first six months of its existence, and it was he who, as Attorney General, ordered the wiretap on Martin Luther King.

Character is destiny. The one adjective inseparable from the name of John F. Kennedy was "young," and since he was young, he had time to wait. But he did not have the inclination. In his column in *The Herald Tribune* for July 31, 1959, Joseph Alsop reported that "The Gallup Poll has just given a Democratic ticket composed of Adlai Stevenson and Senator John F. Kennedy a whopping 56 per cent of the vote." Even his admirers conceded that Kennedy as Senator had held aloof and not really been part of things, but he rejected out of hand the suggestion that he prepare himself for the White House by first serving an apprenticeship under Stevenson. He believed that, like the goddess Minerva, he had sprung full-panoplied from the brow of Jove. If he had had the patience and humility to postpone till a more suitable moment his bid for the Presidency, he and his brother would probably still be alive.

Kennedy seemed to me to be reactive rather than active. Stung by the arrogance of the steel industry—on the occasion when those gentry contemptuously flung down the gaunt-let—he responded with forthright measures; but in terms of family background and early psychological conditioning, it was not his job to *do* anything in the Presidency—it was just his job to *be* there. In the December 9, 1963, issue of *The New Leader*, George E. Herman, White House corre-spondent for CBS News, wrote as follows:

> One day when the late President was a student at Har-vard, his family picked him up for a ride home, and he hap-

pened to bring along a friend and classmate who was from a family well entrenched in Boston's formidable high society. During the course of the ride, Mrs. Rose Kennedy turned to the friend and, with a sort of desperation, said, "Tell me, when are the nice people of Boston going to accept us?" History does not record what must have been the polite and fumbling answer, but the import of the question is clear. Throughout Kennedy's youth his family felt itself to be on the outside; wealthy and powerful though his father had grown, they were still struggling to get in.

The Kennedys as national leaders suffered, I thought, from divided attention. Spiritually, they always had their heads turned back over their shoulders to see whether "the ice-cold Unitarians of Beacon Street" were at last taking notice of them. The publicity about glamour and style and Camelot and being aristocrats convinced nearly everybody except the people who most needed to be convinced by it—the Kennedys themselves. At bottom, they were neurotic and compulsive. And pathetic.

So what? So are a lot of other people. In 1952, when Adlai Stevenson was defeated, some of the political writers said it was Stevenson's tragedy to have been the wrong man in the wrong place at the wrong time. My feeling, however, was that it was John F. Kennedy in the early sixties who was the wrong man, etc. Kennedy had inherited from his predecessor a Caucasian public which had been so much indulged in its race prejudice that Eisenhower had finally been forced to send troops in to Little Rock. He had inherited a public which was punch-drunk and disoriented by the ravages of McCarthyism.

These people needed a long, slow, careful education in responsibility. They needed a leader who could teach them humility because he had it himself. It was insane to think that the damage done by Eisenhower in eight years could be repaired in a few months by a young man in a hurry, even though he surrounded himself with advisers who were always described as vigorous, intelligent and civilized.

However, trying to get anything into print that deglamorized the Kennedys, when their reputation was at its height, was like trying to crack the sound barrier with a slingshot. If you wanted to remark that the Kennedys used liberalism like nail polish, you could only say it in the kind of magazines which do not pay contributors.

"I don't know," I said gloomily to Joseph, upon completing a piece that put the Kennedys into what I thought was the proper perspective, "whether I should send this to my agent or just seal it in a bottle and throw it into Long Island Sound.

"It might," I added, brightening, "wash up on the beach at Hyannis."

Nevertheless, I refused to be discouraged, and this was in part because intuition told me that I was *supposed* to be discouraged. So in the early 1960s I started working on *The Pseudo-Ethic*. Since this book picked up and carried on from where I had left off ten years earlier in *The Folks at Home*, it was clearly not going to make me everybody's favorite character in fact or fiction. But I wanted to survey events and try to find the underlying pattern, even if there was no remotest chance of having what the television people call "impact." There would be no chance of reaching anybody at all if I fell silent and wrote nothing. Furthermore, the very act of writing forced me to clarify my thinking and to distill out of the merely vague the specific, the particular and the graspable.

George Macaulay Trevelyan said that politics is the outcome, not the cause, of social change, and the theme of *The Pseudo-Ethic* was that much in American life which was passing as "merely" political was in fact socioeconomic in origin.

At the end of World War II—so ran the argument—the United States had been left with a huge industrial plant whose staggering output was no longer being used up in armed conflict. At the same time, the American electorate had been trained to have an almost phobic distrust of anything resembling a planned economy. The war-swollen industrial plant, therefore, was not going to be whittled down by government policy to fit the needs of the people. Rather, the needs of the people would have to be stimulated by all kinds of frenetic means until they could absorb the output of industry.

Only one thing stood in the way.

While the United States had been a producing rather than a consuming nation, it had been puritan in outlook and its official morality had been the Judeo-Christian ethic. But that ethic—even in its customary place out in left field— would have been an obstacle to the growth of the consuming society and it was therefore necessary to invalidate it.

But how do you invalidate an ethic?

Not, certainly, by telling people to make themselves slack, greedy and tolerant of evil. The only way to invalidate an ethic is to substitute another ethic—or rather, what *appears* to be another ethic. And this is what was done. The new, substitute ethic—the pseudo-ethic—was anti-Communism, and it was in my view far from being a simple partisan-political phenomenon.

Politics was the medium through which the pseudo-ethic was originally put over, and then like the cuckoo it shouldered the traditional ethic, with all its restraints and disciplines, out of the nest. The irresistible convincer, in the implanting of the pseudo-ethic, was that the country was imperiled by a Communist conspiracy. In 1959 Benjamin Guinzburg, for two years Research Director for the Senate

Subcommittee on Constitutional Rights, published a book called *Rededication to Freedom,* in which he said, "It is time all of us realized that the Communist menace . . . is a naked hoax." But by 1959 the warning came too late.

The pseudo-ethic which supplanted the older traditional ethic appeared to me to have four distinguishing characteristics.

First, it looked down rather than up for authority and sanction. The lives and works of superior people—Abraham Lincoln, Saint Francis of Assisi, Albert Schweitzer, the list is endless—were no longer determinants of value. Popularity, and popularity alone, determined what was acceptable. If enough people told the pollsters that they saw nothing wrong with cannibalism, then cannibalism became a good thing, whatever may have been thought of it previously.

Second, it was consistently vague and evasive and depended a great deal on communication-by-default. President Eisenhower, in the many stands he failed to take, promulgated the pseudo-ethic just as effectively as if he had emblazoned on the White House in letters of fire, "Inertia, be thou my guide. Cowardice, be thou my watchword."

Third, it often held up as desirable behavior what were in effect crazy inversions of the traditional ethic. The leitmotif of the whole anti-Communist hysteria was that a man was guilty until proved innocent, and wide sections of the American public came to feel at that time that where any kind of supposedly left-wing belief was involved, injustice was not only forgivable but actually rather more desirable as a goal than justice itself.

Fourth, the pseudo-ethic was indissolubly linked to anti-Communism as a domestic issue. The paradox of the convulsive anti-Communism which kept the United States in its grip for so long was that—loudly proclaiming ourselves as in every way distinct from, and immeasurably superior to, the Russians—we were in fact tied to them in a degrading kind of dependence.

If the Russians had political purges and executed people, then it was all right for us to have *Red Channels* and the Hollywood blacklist. If the Soviet government had in the 1930s allowed four million peasants to starve, in order to break resistance to collectivization, that meant we did not have to do much about black Americans being second-class citizens because what we were doing to black citizens was not as bad as what the Russians had done to the kulaks. Morally, we operated in a Russian frame of reference and not in the one native to us.

To be sure, the Judeo-Christian ethic was itself an imperfect instrument of social control. Way back in the 1920s, Norman Douglas in his then-famous book *South Wind*, had called it "that quaint Alexandrian tutti-frutti." Its sexual taboos are out of line with human nature as, with the advance of knowledge, we have come to know human nature. But when Freudian insights, plus the wide dissemination of contraceptives, made the Biblical injunctions about chastity obsolete, it did not mean that honesty, loyalty and a sense of responsibility for others also became obsolete and irrelevant to the conduct of human affairs.

Herbert J. Muller, in his book *The Uses of the Past*, noted that the prophets of the Judeo-Christian ethic have been conspicuous among the religious leaders of mankind for the eloquence of their protest against social injustice. To discard that ethic *in toto* because one part of it—its sexual code—has not survived the erosion of Time was to throw out the baby with the bath.

Similarly, the traditional ethic postulated an anthropomorphic God, but when that celestial worthy had to gather up his draperies and scuttle out of the way of astronauts, it did not invalidate morality. The justification—the *raison d'être*—of morality is not an imaginary Deity who wants us all to be virtuous and who will punish those who are not. The *raison d'être* of a stable moral standard—widely agreed upon, and reinforced when necessary by suitable punishment—is that it results in predictable behavior. The guests do not read the letters on the desk. The Mansons do not murder Sharon Tate.

Of course, the traditional ethic was not openly, unashamedly, and officially junked in the interests of the consuming society. Nobody would have stood for that. It was merely assigned to second place. Honesty and fair play were still goals to aim at, but if you were "staunchly anti-Communist," you were automatically given absolution for anything tricky or unsavory in your record because anti-Communism as a virtue outranked honesty and scrupulousness. The catch, however, was that an ethic will not work if it is known by everybody to have been relegated to second place. It has to be in the top slot, or it becomes ineffective as an instrument of social control.

Nobody, of course, sat down and deliberately planned to substitute a pseudo-ethic for the traditional one. Shaw points out in his Preface to *Saint Joan* that whatever Joan of Arc herself may have thought, she was actually a secular agent who was bringing an end to feudalism and paving the way for the nation-state. The Affluence Peddlers were only the most conspicuous exemplars of a whole tribe, and they were all of them unwitting agents of an overriding secular process— namely, the mongrelization of ethics.

The Pseudo-Ethic concluded by saying:

> The idealist deals with facts quite as much as the realist. He merely sees them differently, and it is that difference of viewpoint which we have had to live without for some

years now. A more intimate relationship exists between the ideal and the "real" than it is currently fashionable to acknowledge. That relationship consists of the quintessential practicality of the ideal, and it was probably never better expressed than by Dr. A. J. Muste when he described utopianism as "the growing edge of society."

Indeed it is.

The Pseudo-Ethic came out in 1963, and while it did not meet with quite so chilling a silence as had greeted *The Folks at Home*, the response to it was rather more the ripple than the neap tide. After its publication, I wrote a few magazine articles, mostly in connection with the civil rights movement of the 1960s, but I did not do another book until I began this one in the early 1970s. This was because of several totally unforeseen developments in my personal life. By this time well into my fifties, I had assumed that for the rest of my span on earth, all I had to do was coast home. Life, however, had decided that it was time for me to have one last and supreme force-feeding.

9
The Center Does Not Hold

In 1964 Angus Cotter died and I failed to notice—or rather, to see the significance of—something that I was later to realize had been a portent. For twenty years Joseph's and my marriage had had in the background Joseph's good relationship with Angus. As commander and brilliant second-in-command, Dr. Cotter and Joseph had given their school an enviable reputation in its field. Nevertheless, when Angus died, Joseph—though he was energetic and practical and of great help to the Cotter family—showed no sign of grief. To me, at least. He was appropriately unsmiling, but the event did not seem to have the impact on him that I would have expected.

In the early years of our marriage, I used to ask my husband questions about himself—about his childhood and the girls he had gone out with when he was young and about his political idealism when he was in college—but he always made some quick, evasive reply and turned the conversation back to me and my problems. Which did not mortally offend me. By the time Angus Cotter died, I had long outgrown the minimal curiosity I had originally had about what made Joseph tick.

Though he did not visibly mourn Dr. Cotter's passing as I had thought he would, he nevertheless scoured the country to find somebody else in the field of education with whom he could have the same relationship. Angus Cotter, however, had been unique, and finally in 1966 Joseph took a job in a midwestern city, as head of a school where, instead of being second-in-command, he was to have sole responsibility for an enterprise of considerable dimensions. We moved to the Middle West in June of 1966, immediately after Celia had been graduated from high school. Celia as she grew up had turned out to be gifted artistically, and in September she left for London to study at the Slade School of Fine Arts.

Joseph and I had been Eastern Seaboard people all our lives and we were both daunted at the prospect of living in America's heartland. Especially without our daughter. In addition, we had friends of many years' standing in both New York and Westchester, and removal from their neighborhood was going to be keenly felt. The most conspicuous alteration in our life pattern, however, was that Joseph would for the first time be on his own, professionally.

I thought that the most valuable contribution I could make to the new venture would be to get over the alcoholic rages, so that he would not have that particular albatross hanging around his neck. By this time I had been psychoanalyzed so often that I had a feeling my personality might disappear through a sheer superabundance of therapy—like a substance ground into such fine particles that a breath of wind would blow it away. Nevertheless, I started going to yet another analyst for the purpose of putting an end to those unpredictable bouts of being "abused and abusive."

Bulldogs have been known to fall on their swords when confronted by my superior tenacity, and by the end of the year I had accomplished what I had set out to accomplish.

Dr. S.—another Dr. S.—was like Dr. J. in having both intuition and empathy, and we got along like the traditional
house afire.

"What does the psychiatrist do," I asked, "in the ten
minutes he allows himself between patients? He has an itch
between his shoulder blades and looks around exhaustively
for a pencil with which to scratch it, but he cannot find one,
so he goes to the mirror which hangs in his little private
washroom and pulls his jaw down and to one side while he
examines a blemish on his cheek. When he is satisfied that it
is unnoticeable, he looks at his watch, sees what time it is,
puts on his 'Nothing-you-say-can-shock-me' expression and
opens the door for the next human wreck."

Newton Arvin says in his critique of Herman Melville
that Melville showed all his life a pattern of retaliation for injury; and in the sessions with Dr. S., we gradually worked it
out that the rages were not a response to my present-day situation, desperately though I tried to make them seem so. They
came from a still-unresolved relationship with Annie, and
were the expression of an implacable and devouring fury with
her because I had laid at her feet every gift in my command
and she had responded with indifference and inattention.

The hard lesson I had to learn—and it *was* hard—was
that you cannot go back when you are grown up and punish
your parents for what they did to you when you were a child.
I do not believe I would have been able to learn this lesson
save for the fact that by that time I had not seen or heard
from my mother for eight years and the hold she had on me
had therefore been weakened.

But though I succeeded in weaning myself from the
habit of harking back to the unredeemable past, I did not
drink less. Not much less, at any rate. For years I had been
saying to myself every morning, "Tonight I will have only
two drinks before I go to bed," and some nights I actually

did. But on other nights I sat up alone—sometimes for an hour or two, sometimes for many hours.

Stony-faced and nursing a fistful of Scotch, I stared into the fireplace while inside my head a rich fantasy life went on in which all remembered and brooded-upon defeats to the ego were turned into unequivocal triumphs. But now— although I still could not go to sleep until every shred of emotional discomfort had been dissolved away with revisionist imaginings—I could at least be sure that the third or fourth drink would not trigger off one of those paroxysms of frustration where I threw my glass at that same fireplace and shattered it without the formality of saying, "Gentlemen, the Queen!"

The city to which we had moved was not exactly sweet Auburn, fairest village of the plain. Though it was the home of one of America's key industries, it was in outward appearance as gray and dreary and inert as the elastic on a worn-out brassiere. However, Joseph seemed, so far as a wife could tell, to be responding very ably to the demands of the new job—though he was, for him, unwontedly silent. He no longer took care of me in the solicitous way he had formerly done, but I had known before we went there that, with his enlarged responsibility, he could not be expected to.

A compulsive accepter of challenges, I had made up my mind that, insofar as it depended on me, Joseph and I were going to have a good life in our new place of residence. We had a beautiful apartment which I had fixed up with great care, and by the end of the first year I thought it could safely be said that self and helpmeet were modestly flourishing despite our changed circumstances.

And then a blow fell which was totally unanticipated. Celia came home from England for her summer vacation pale and listless, and two weeks after her return, she suddenly developed double vision. We took her to a doctor and the diagnosis was shattering. Brain tumor. An exploratory operation was performed and the tumor was pronounced to be inoperable. The doctors minced words, but conveyed through circumlocutions that although she might get well enough to go back for another year at the Slade, she was earmarked for the Grim Reaper.

Norman Mailer once said that nothing shows up the weakness in a marriage like having a sick child. The day we brought Celia home after the brain surgery, I got her settled in bed and walked into the dining room to find Joseph looking out of the window. Without turning around, he said, "I want you to go to New York and take a little apartment and write. I don't want you here."

I thought the shock of Celia's illness must have driven him temporarily out of his mind. Our daughter was in the room across the hall with one large and two small holes in the back of her head, and she was not going to be with us for very much longer.

"You need a drink," I said.

But the following week he said without preamble, "I want a divorce."

To say this came as a shock is the understatement of the century. It was as if Leonard Woolf had suddenly told Virginia to get lost. All through the years of our marriage— when I heard other women complaining that their husbands drank too much or were unfaithful or never read a book— I thought of Joseph's and my interwovenness and maintained a silence which I hoped was conspicuous. That interwovenness, in a world where all the landmarks were disintegrating with appalling rapidity, had seemed the one perdurable thing.

When my speech centers recovered from their paralysis, I finally managed to say, "Why?"

"I don't have to give any reasons," he said. "It's enough that I want one."

"*Now?* What about Celia?"

"She's nineteen. Children that age don't care what their parents do."

The year that followed was unbelievable. It simply could not be happening, and yet it was. Joseph never let up. He would not sit down and discuss the matter. He would not go to a marriage counselor. Above all, he would not elucidate.

"I haven't a shred of a case," he used to say as he went off to work in the morning, "but that isn't going to make any difference.

"All the cards are in your hands, but don't think you can stop me."

Meantime, Celia was going through an interminable medical purgatory—doctors, doctors, doctors, pathologists, internists, specialists, tests, pills, injections, consultations, diagnostic drugs—the whole modern arsenal of weapons that can be invoked against disease. At Christmas, six months after the first operation, she had a second one which it was hoped would alleviate a severe pain she had developed in her back, but it failed of its objective. Hopes rose and then collapsed and then rose again.

Joseph, however, continued on his chosen course. Not all the time. There were lulls and temporary breathing spells. Sometimes he would say, "I won't leave you until Celia goes back to the Slade." Though I thought his behavior monstrous, it was not monstrous if you granted his basic premise. That premise was that since Celia had not borne a child out of wedlock and was not hooked on heroin, she was emotionally secure and nothing he might do could disturb her. In this conviction, he was unshakable, and no matter what I said or how I said it, he just smiled and walked away.

In that year there was a race riot in the city to which we had moved. It took place more or less under our windows, so that it seemed as if the outside world had raised to some astronomical power the dissension that was taking place at home.

It was a nightmare, but it was a nightmare made worse than it need have been by the (unperceived) limitations of my own character, and the real victim, of course, was my daughter. To face at nineteen the prospect of extinction—to be living in constant pain, plus the vertigo and nausea that go with any disturbance of the brain centers—and on top of that to have your parents, whose supplemental harmony you have been used to all your life, suddenly start acting like two tarantulas in a bottle . . . and all this in a strange city where you are far away from the friends you have grown up with and the familiar house where you spent your whole childhood . . .

When I look back on my life, the most shameful blot on my escutcheon is that in her hour of greatest need, I failed my daughter. I took good care of her physical requirements, but she did not have my real attention. Blinded by egotistic fury at Joseph's astonishing rejection of me, I ministered to her wants punctiliously but mechanically, and the worst thing of all was that I even had fleeting seconds of being grateful for her illness, because if it came to the crunch vis-à-vis divorce, it really did put all the cards in my hands. I was—though at the time I considered myself a noble character outrageously wronged—basically just as self-indulgent as my husband.

In a money-and-success society, selflessness is the most suspect of all the virtues. Nobody can believe that it is anything but a front for some kind of racket. But had I been capable of a self-forgetful concern for my daughter, I would have been less vulnerable to the incredible change, in Joseph's attitude toward me, from a loving and cherishing admiration to total enmity. I would have been able to see that this scarifying situation could not have developed unless the potential for it had always existed.

Joseph had been used to say that it was very important to him in our marriage that I was the keeper of his conscience. I had felt proud to be assigned this responsibility, and had not stopped to think that conscience is one thing which above all else should be entirely in one's own charge. He had also on a few occasions said, in moments of depression, "I don't feel real." I had paid no attention, because it was not a feeling I ever had myself, and what I could not relate to myself, I was incurious about.

Nobody's behavior is inexplicable, if you have sufficient data and the wit—plus the inclination—to interpret it properly. In that vertiginous first year of our daughter's illness, I was so busy luxuriating in the posture of injured innocent that it did not occur to me to review the data and subject Joseph's behavior—and my own—to intelligent scrutiny. The one question I should have asked myself was, "Did I deserve this treatment?" The answer would have been that I did. I was reaping the whirlwind because I had sowed the wind some three years earlier, although by the time we moved to the Middle West I had forgotten it.

In 1964, Joseph had been given a six-month sabbatical and we decided to go to England. We were going to take Celia with us and put her in school there. Joseph planned to do research at an English university, and I was going to try to clear my mind of McCarthyism and consumerism and, in a poorer country and a relatively purer political climate, work out what I wanted to say in my next book.

When we announced our plans, Joseph's mother said

she was going to come and visit us. I sealed the doom of my marriage by five carelessly spoken words.

"Tell her not to come," I said.

Joseph had never displayed any particular attachment to his mother, and my purpose in going to England was to get away from America and all reminders of it. I felt an imperious need for a spell of uninterrupted foreignness. Years of uttering fierce protests which are promptly lost in a void can eventually get one down; and whatever my mother-in-law's merits, they were not such as to be of any help to a person who was trying to regroup her spiritual forces. But I did not anticipate any trouble. Joseph had occasionally said, apropos of his mother, "She respects my privacy," and I took it for granted that he would have a quiet word with her and that would be that.

When somebody is hit by overwhelming disaster, it is often possible to discern in the victim some quality or other which invited the disaster. Which may, in fact, have made it inevitable. My disaster-inviting quality was literal-mindedness. It never occurred to me that people might not mean precisely what they said. Or that, if they meant it at the moment, they might not still mean it next week or next year. Whatever I heard spoken aloud I regarded as a commitment on which I could rely forever.

Joseph did not have a quiet word with his mother and that was not that. He approached the situation circuitously. He went to Becky's friends and relatives and urged them to represent to her that we were going to England to work and that our work would suffer if it were interrupted. However, my mother-in-law was, if nothing else, a superb strategist and much too clever to allow herself to be drawn into argument. If it were suggested to her that something she wanted to do was inadvisable, she did not descend to self-justification.

With a self-control far beyond anything I could muster, she merely smiled sweetly and became completely deaf.

The question of Joseph's mother's projected visit became a topic extensively canvassed among our friends, and I remember a discussion we had with a couple who shall be called Bill and Sally.

"How long is she going to stay?" Bill asked equably, for he and Sally were both mild and sweet-tempered people.

I shrugged. "A few days. Maybe only a night or two."

"Well . . ." said Sally smilingly, not feeling it necessary to add, "You're making a mountain out of a molehill."

Only half a dozen words had been exchanged, but I was already in despair. I was fond of these people, and thought they were fond of me, but I could tell from their tone of voice that what to me was a species of rape was to them no more than being bumped into in the street.

"It's not a question of how long she stays," I said. "It's a question of her coming at all."

Dismayed, I sensed both Bill and Sally recoiling from what seemed to them uncalled-for pugnacity, but Sally said coaxingly, "She must be lonely, now that Joseph's father is gone."

"Oh, come! He's been dead for five years."

As a matter of fact, I had been conscientiously supportive and attentive to Becky for a long time after that event, and she had frequently said that she did not know what she would have done without me.

"Do you grudge the poor old lady a trip to Europe and a chance to visit her son?" Bill asked reproachfully.

"Poor old lady!"

Becky's life was a busy round of opera, concerts, theater and other stimulating diversions and she ran more philanthropic organizations than you could shake a stick at. It was like being tied to the railroad track while the bystanders shed tears for the onrushing locomotive.

Only a few nights before, however, another friend had said indignantly, "Who does she think she is, to go crashing in on a writer who has gone away to work? Read her the riot act!"

I was just taking heart from this recollection when Sally said, "After all, she's Joseph's *mother*."

"That," I snapped, "was not a very difficult position to achieve."

Joseph, who had been keeping uncharacteristically silent, spoke for the first time. "She's very generous," he said.

"Yes, I know. She'll bring us expensive presents and she'll insist on taking us for some lovely jaunt to France or Ireland that we couldn't afford ourselves. But I fear the Greeks bearing gifts."

I heard my voice being shrill and unruly and knew that I was in my usual position of failing to convince through being too emotional. But Joseph, who for years had been explaining to people the idiosyncratic needs of writers, was this time conspicuously not doing so.

"The real generosity," I said, "would be to leave us alone."

"Couldn't you make a sacrifice?" Bill asked.

"Because Joseph makes a lot of sacrifices for me? Yes, I could. I'm not a monster."

A certain something in the air suggested that this claim was not going to be allowed, but I pressed on.

"If we were just going to Europe on a junket, I'd put up with it, though Becky has been to Europe a million times and there's no need for her to go now. But Joseph and I are going abroad to work."

I looked at my husband.

" 'You shall not press down upon the brow of Labor this crown of thorns.' "

To my great relief, Joseph laughed, but Sally, gravely reproachful, said, "She'll come, and it will be a nuisance, but she'll go away again and you'll forget all about it."

"No!"

Eyes widened.

"This isn't a purblind little old lady making an innocent mistake. This is a probing operation by a hellishly determined woman."

This time Bill and Sally really did recoil.

"Nonsense!" and "That's utterly farfetched!" they exclaimed in concert, and Joseph's lips tightened.

I felt as if the Incas were cutting my heart out with a stone knife, but I knew as surely as I knew that two and two are four that if we did not fight this out with Becky right then, it would only have to be fought out another time.

"You're arguing," I said passionately, "on the theory of virtue through satiety. It's like Hitler and the Sudetenland. Give the aggressor what he wants, and that makes him satisfied and peaceful forever after."

I swallowed.

"But it never works out that way. Never."

The word "aggressor" had jolted them, and I was suddenly and piercingly reminded of the fights I had had with Reinhold about having dates when I was in high school. To my father, those South Yonkers high school boys had been cynical libertines, and with exactly the same skewed-up vision, Joseph's mother was, to my present antagonists, a self-effacing Mater Dolorosa who would not know a power play from a maiden's swoon.

Addressing myself to Joseph, I fired the last shot in my locker.

" 'The loving is in the letting go.' "

It was a favorite line of his from W. H. Auden, and it softened him.

He smiled.

"It will work out," he said easily, and deftly switched the conversation to another subject.

When we sailed for England, my mother-in-law was still being blandly noncommittal, but we hoped that she would in the end bow to the pressure that was being exerted on her. However, we had not been at the English university very long before we got a letter from her, postmarked London, which began, "Hi, darlings! Here I am!"

I exploded. "If you let that woman come here," I said, "I'm taking the next ship back to the United States."

"Handle it yourself," Joseph said sullenly.

I wrote Becky the kind of letter that Harry Truman used to send to the music critics who said his daughter could not sing, and she went back to the States without seeing us.

How did it happen that this bit of family drama developed so unexpectedly in Joseph's and my life together? One can only speculate, but it seems to me possible that it arose from nothing more consequential than the fact that my mother-in-law was bored. The family firm had been sold when Joseph's father died, and busy though she kept herself, her various activities did not suffice to use up all of her phenomenal supply of energy. So what better way to introduce a bit of excitement into life than to assert a hegemony over her son's marriage?

However, the venture failed—from her point of view—and all would have been well save for the fact that I was furious with Joseph and clobbered him for months thereafter with scorn and reproach. I was furious because I thought he was afraid of his mother. Heaven knew, I had been abjectly terrified of mine. I was furious because for twenty years he had represented himself as not being afraid of her. People who are very hard on themselves—as Reinhold had been about getting to be an architect, and I had been about not giving in to the phobia—are unfortunately apt to be equally hard on others, and the others sometimes fail to appreciate the austere beauty of the standards which are being ruthlessly imposed upon them.

Cold sober or inflamed with Scotch, I did not let Joseph forget my conviction that he had passed himself off as something he was not. I had what the French call *déformation professionelle*. I did not realize that the polemic which looks so dazzling in *The New Republic* is contraindicated, as the medical fellows say, for domestic use. At home, one must learn to be right quietly. And only once. Joseph made no attempt to defend himself against these taunts. He received them in silence. And after a while—a long while—even I considered the subject exhausted and dropped it. But that was the background—though it had all passed completely out of my mind by the time we got to the Middle West—for my husband's suddenly saying he wanted a divorce.

Despite having nothing to rely on but her own will to survive, our daughter gradually got better during that winter of 1967–68, although when I think of how often, during the years when she was growing up, her father and I congratulated ourselves on what good parents we were, it is appalling to realize how completely, when it really mattered, we both let her down. But she had the kind of courage that Reinhold must have had when he went through in total isolation his post-retirement breakdown, and in September of 1968 she was well enough to go back to the Slade. Joseph and I were united in a common joy that she should have made such a good recovery and a common anxiety about having her so far away. I was thus unprepared, a few days after her departure, to come home from my shopping and find a note from him Scotch-taped to the wall in the foyer of our apartment.

"I have decided to leave you," it said.

10

Coming In on a Wing and a Prayer

It would seem as if nothing could be easier to write than autobiography. You just sit down and tell what happened, starting at the beginning and proceeding to the end. In reality, however, one is balanced on a knife edge all the time between being cursory and/or evasive on the one hand or long-windedly self-important on the other. The breaking up of a marriage, when it is not by mutual consent, is especially perilous to describe; but nothing venture, nothing gain.

When I found Joseph's note, I erupted into Hotspur-type behavior. Many years before, Tom Stix had reminded me of the Code—the Code being that one delivers this kind of message in person and not in writing. I did not stop to think that I myself had needed to be reminded of the Code and that Joseph did not have any Tom Stix.

I went to the bar of the hotel next door, drank four old-fashioneds, came home and scooped up all of Joseph's clothes I could carry in both arms and took them to Goodwill Industries. It was certainly my evil genius which inspired that particular gesture. If Joseph had had a library of priceless old books and I had dropped them one by one down the incinerator shaft of our apartment building, he might in the long run have forgiven me, but to dispose of his wardrobe thus cavalierly was in his view an act of unexampled malevolence.

For the next two months, I did not see him or hear from him, though a check arrived every week for my living expenses. I had supposedly finished my work with Dr S., but all the people who had known Joseph and me for a long time were back East, so I kept on seeing Dr. S. because there was nobody else to talk to. Dr. S. advised against my trying to get in touch with Joseph. "Let him play out his string," he said. "Whatever it is."

During the years of Joseph's and my marriage, I had had a good deal of what airline pilots call "turbulence," but I had never been lonely. There had always been Celia and Joseph to take care of and make a home for, and in the case of Joseph, to apply to for comfort, reassurance and advice. Those two months were my introduction to loneliness. They would have been painful to anybody, but they were excruciating to me because I had always unconsciously thought myself too special and privileged a person to have to share in the common human experience of forlornness. It was part of the force-feeding, however, and perhaps eventually resulted in widening—at least in some small degree—sympathies which to start with were rather narrow.

Very shortly after Joseph's departure, a kindly man of my acquaintance took me to lunch and told me that I ought to have a lawyer, and as we said good-bye, on the pavement outside the restaurant, he added one last comment.

"You know," he said gravely, "you have committed the worst crime in the book."

I stared at him aghast.

"You haven't any money," he said.

Nor did I. From the day we were married, I had turned

all the money I earned over to Joseph and never given it a
further thought. But where my acquaintance had spoken
ironically, the lawyer who was secured for me said the same
thing, and without a trace of irony. A tall man, this lawyer
was thin and hard and very clean, like a freshly covered ironing board. I had not been in his office ten minutes when he
said reproachfully, "You were extremely foolish ever to let
your husband lay his hands on a penny of your earnings.
You should have put them aside in case of just this kind of
situation."

"But what sort of household would it have been for my
daughter to grow up in," I countered hotly, "if I had been so
suspicious of her father that I kept all my money to myself?"

The lawyer was no more responsive to this argument
than that domestic appurtenance he so closely resembled,
and he adverted to the matter, with a rueful shake of the
head, on several occasions thereafter.

But I needed his services, because almost immediately
after my first interview with him, he telephoned to say that
Joseph had served me with divorce papers.

"You don't need to be divorced if you don't want to be,"
he said in his computerlike way. "There's no case."

Morally speaking, there was a case against me, but it
was not one that could have been proved in court with witnesses, since wild horses would never have made me hector
Joseph outside the bosom of the family. The Ironing Board
himself thought there was a case against me, but he thought
the case against me was that I was too old. He intimated,
through a series of unfinished sentences, that no American
male who was doing as well in his career as Joseph ought to
be encumbered with a hunk of protoplasm of the female per-
suasion who had passed the menopause.

I was fifty-eight, but I did not *feel* old. I was, in fact, so
full of adrenalin that any well-advised general staff would

have selected me above all others to lead the Charge of the Light Brigade. But the Ironing Board left me in no doubt that his concept of the ideal client was a lady who arrived in his office with a fistful of greenbacks in one hand and a box of Tampax in the other.

At the time these events were taking place, I was not analytical about them, but in retrospect they seem to have been colored all along the way by the money-and-success standard. My mother-in-law had certainly not consciously planned to wreak the havoc she did by her ill-judged trip to England. However, being herself a successful businesswoman, she probably assumed that since I was no longer "a famous author," I regarded myself as a failure. She therefore expected to find me pulpy and anticipated no more resistance than would make life temporarily exciting.

But it was a case of the irresistible force meeting the immovable object, because I did not regard myself as a failure. I felt I had suffered an undeserved neglect, and my little household was thoroughly conversant with my complaints on that score. But I would only have considered myself a failure if somebody had come along and demolished my arguments. My mother-in-law and I had been on terms too formal for her to realize that I had been stamped with the imprint of an old-fashioned Civil Service background. In that milieu, you knew before you started in on your career that whatever satisfactions it might ultimately vouchsafe, making a pile of money was not going to be one of them. Not, at least, if you had scruples.

With the advantage of hindsight, something else becomes obvious which entirely escaped me at the time—to wit, that family patterns repeat themselves from generation to generation unless they are consciously interrupted. My father had been determined to make me into a lady banker, and after he had been dead for years, I tried with the same nonacceptance of reality to make Joseph into the one Jewish boy in New York who was not afraid of his mother. And just as I was my father all over again, Joseph seemed to be his mother all over again. Wishing to do something to which, conceivably, objections might be raised, he declined to argue and would not stoop to self-justification. He merely smiled and became deaf.

After two months of being alone in our large apartment, I realized that if I did not do something to alter the situation, I would crack under the strain. So I decided to go to London for six months. Celia was there; and both Dr. S. and I believed that if I were far away, Joseph might have second thoughts. Consequently, it was arranged between his lawyer and the Ironing Board that he would give me money to fly to England, although Joseph insisted on the proviso that if he still wanted a divorce after six months, I would agree to it.

It seemed to me that, in view of our daughter's illness, we should not take so drastic a step as divorce unless we had first tried living together again. If Joseph would tell me what he wanted, I would try to give it to him, and only if I proved unable to do so, should the marriage be dissolved. But Joseph could not see that anything drastic was involved. "Divorce is nothing," he said. "It's just a joke. Nobody takes it seriously any more."

I went to London and for the first three months there, I appeared to be out of the frying pan, into the fire. Accommodation was scarce, and the only place I could find to live in was a cold, damp, basement apartment whose charnel-house atmosphere was so striking that as soon as you crossed the threshold, you looked around for the bones. Although the place was not cheap, the furniture was skimpy, makeshift and depressing. Furthermore, the rooms were impossible to heat—but this provided a very tolerable excuse for warming oneself up with Scotch.

As I recollect it now, I had only been in England a few weeks when Joseph wrote to say that if I did not consent to an immediate divorce, he would stop sending me money to live on. I did not have a separation-and-support agreement, so I had no protection against this threat and the Ironing Board did not reply to my frantic letters. Actually he did not stop sending the money, so I suppose the letter was a mere ploy, but I reacted to it as if it were for real and went through agonies of fear and helpless rage. Though I did not realize it at the time, I had been betrayed once again by literal-mindedness.

The first three months in England were a sort of do-it-yourself Götterdammerung, but at last the instinct for survival began to break through. I came to the end of years of mental sidestepping and realized that I would have to stop drinking.

"The drinking is only a small part of our life together," Joseph had once written me when he was away somewhere. "I am thinking tonight of your great and sweeping loyalties. . . ."

But I was now alone, and that meant I was down to bedrock. The keynote of my personality had always been dependence, and the obvious symbol of that dependence was alcohol. For years I had comforted myself by thinking that—although I did not seem able to stick to a mere two drinks after dinner—at least I did not smash cars into traffic standards or get into fights in bars. I had tried to compromise by curing myself of the rages, and this last might have been sufficient as long as I lived in an attractive apartment and was buttressed by domestic responsibilities and a helpful psychiatrist. But by myself in a cryptlike set of rooms in London, I was confronted with a specter that almost literally made my hair stand on end.

Thanks to Annie's tutelage, I had all my life been a slave to what people might think of me—another form of dependence and one which had often earned my daughter's scorn. If I went on with my solitary drinking, however, it was quite conceivable that I could reach a point where I no longer cared what people might think of me. Recoil is scarcely the word for my response to this prospect. You can, to paraphrase the old saying, take the girl out of Lincoln Park, but you cannot take Lincoln Park out of the girl.

I did stop drinking. Susan Sontag once referred, in an article in *The Partisan Review,* to "strident self-transcenders and spiritual athletes"—a phrase which I read at the time with a wincing awareness that it might apply to me. But if you are giving up a long-established bad habit, it helps to be a prig. I did not try to cushion the deprivation with tranquilizers, because they too are a symbol of dependence. London itself, however, was a kind of tranquilizer. It had been there for so long. It was so full of memories of "old, unhappy, far-off things, and battles long ago." People had been beheaded on Tower Hill, hanged at Tyburn for stealing a loaf of bread and only yesterday killed in the blitz. Against such a background, how important was one American divorce?

Rage and happiness.

I had had enough of the latter in my life to be convinced that the one indispensable ingredient of human happiness is growth. But for the personality whose native hue is obsession, the addictive use of alcohol inhibits growth. Employed as I had been employing it, liquor is a fixative of old patterns; and the old patterns in my case were literal-mindedness, impetuosity, vengefulness and violence, and above all a tender, solicitous concern for self. (The latter having indubitably been strengthened by the success of *With Malice.*)

I cannot, now, write about the mental rehabilitation that became possible, once I had stopped relying on alcohol, without making it sound much neater and more orderly than it actually was. The Education of Margaret Halsey did not proceed apace, and it must often have seemed to a casual observer that it was not proceeding at all. It was a progression of two steps forward and one step back, and I was destined to impale myself once again on the stake of literal-mindedness.

When I at long last heard from the Ironing Board, he was not the bearer of glad tidings. Joseph, he informed me, was proposing to cut by a third the amount of alimony which had been requested, and was also proposing that I should only receive alimony for the next ten years. For a woman of fifty-nine, this was scarcely a cuddly outlook—and once again I did not recognize a mere gambit when I saw it.

I got the lawyer's letter in the late afternoon, and the night that followed was a pure Gethsemane. Fear and fury surged about inside me like the sixty-foot tides in the Bay of Fundy, but I clung blindly to one idea—*not* to reach for the bottle of Scotch. I drank coffee, and when my nerves were shrieking with overstimulation from that innocuous beverage, I took aspirin. Then I ate slices of dry bread to keep from getting sick from the aspirin. After which, I started over again on the coffee.

But the one idea I tried not to lose hold of was a semantic one—i.e., that when I spoke of having *a* drink, it was a euphemism for having a whole flock of them. I knew that if I so much as smelled a cork, I would end up by telephoning Joseph in the United States and telling him what I thought of him, and he would be able to say, "She called me from London, drunk as a skunk, and was abusive." If I died for it, he was not going to have that triumph.

"Even the old can learn," says the defeated tyrant Creon

at the end of Sophocles' *Antigone*. The first lesson I had to
master was that there was a world of difference between what
I wanted and what I needed. What I wanted was a great,
smashing vindication of myself as a wife, but what I needed
was, in the phrase of one of the German philosophers, to
carry the torch to the back of the cave. The debacle which
appeared to have descended on me with such mysterious sud-
denness had in actuality long roots in the past.

The two most significant people in Joseph's life for the
preceding twenty-five years had been Angus Cotter and myself. Dr. Cotter and I were both of Scottish extraction; we
were both Puritans; and we were both physically Anglo-
Saxon types. Perhaps both those relationships had been
based, for Joseph, on the principle of "If you can't lick 'em,
join 'em." But given a choice, he would rather have licked
'em. Who wouldn't? Perhaps it was this enforced identification to which he was giving expression when he said, "I don't
feel real."

Angus Cotter was a much more temperate person than
either my father or I. Reinhold and I, however, had always
unconsciously preened ourselves on smashing through to our
objectives, with our high principles snapping in the breeze
like the pennons on an ocean liner. No deviousness for us.
No wily manipulations behind the scenes. Just the manly,
straightforward clout with the mace. It had never occurred to
either my father or me that we smashed through because we
could afford to, since we belonged to what was up until
recently the dominant group in the culture.

It must have seemed to my mother-in-law, for instance,
that I had never really had to work for what I got. And in
terms of the obstacles which, in my father's and my generations, were placed in the way of minorities, she was right. It
may also have seemed to her—though perhaps she never put
it into so many words—that a person who is brought up as a

child to be anti-Semitic never really gets over it. In this, too—if she ever entertained such a notion—I think she was probably right.

If the torch were carried to the back of the cave, what did it illuminate that had previously been obscure? For one thing, it had to be admitted that while both my father and I were respected and relied upon, we were also feared. We were feared because of the violence in both our natures, and this meant that people did not confide in us and we were often unaware of what they were up to. The torch also illuminated something else that one would not, by preference, have chosen to become aware of.

From the very beginning of the marital disaster, I had taken it for granted that I was an injured innocent and the role was one that actors describe as a fat part. But if the injury was agonizing, the innocence was delicious. And it was fake. It could be seen to be fake because I was, in the person of my daughter, in the presence of genuine injured innocence.

Celia's ordeal had left her frail, but she was nevertheless—when I got to London—doing very well in her second year at the Slade. I am a humorist and a polemicist and not a novelist, and only a novelist could hope to portray what it must have meant to my daughter to be struck down simultaneously by the tumor and the breakdown of her parents' marriage. Nobody sustains a double-barreled injury like that without being ravaged inside, but her outward behavior from the very first day of her illness was one of quiet fortitude. Not until she was taken ill did I realize how much people loved and admired her—she had showed great talent as an etcher—and if she had to be summed up in a single word, that word would be one which is not used very much today. Gallant.

But how much did her own mother love her? I had arrived in London determined to fight a holy war (which is the

worst kind) against Joseph's divorce suit. I told myself that
what my daughter needed above all else in this crisis of her
life was to have her parents' marriage kept together in some
form or other, however modified. But what she actually
needed above all else was for me to be less self-absorbed than
I had been during the first year of her illness.

One could only speculate, but it seemed at least conceivable that Joseph, at some deep and soundless level of his
being, had regarded Dr. Cotter's death as an abandonment
and a betrayal. That left me—were this hypothesis accurate—as the only available surrogate upon whom he could
avenge himself for this treachery. Such a theory, if correct,
would account for his inaccessibility to reason, moderation,
and compromise. But it did not absolve me from responsibility for my own share in the breakup of the marriage.

I had been furious because, when Joseph's mother followed us to England, he would not take up the cudgels in
defense of our right to privacy. But if the shoe had been on
the other foot—if Annie had made such a foray during the
years when I compulsively capitulated to her—would I have
got up on my hind legs and said, "Thus far and no farther?"
The conflict between Joseph and me may simply have been a
conflict between two opposing infantilisms, and he had the
edge because he knew me so well—whereas I, it turned out, did
not know him at all.

I had only one recourse. I would have to become someone *he* did not know. Somebody less easily stampeded.
Camus once said that in these troubled times, he wished to
be neither victim nor executioner. If I had killed Joseph's
idea of himself, then I had been an executioner. But I did
not have to be a victim. I did not have to let myself be manipulated into ending up as a dreary and drunken old Burnt-
Out Case.

"Whoever wants to reform the world," said Thoreau,

"had better begin with himself." Reinhold's type of self-made man is now an extinct species, but it was characteristic of such forgers-ahead that they wallowed in self-pity. From my earliest days of infancy, I had been accustomed to hearing my father expound, in accents either choleric or melancholy, on what a hard life he had had, and I had taken over this trait lock, stock and barrel. When I stopped to listen to myself, I could hear exactly the same timbre in my voice that I had been used to hear in his.

Even during the many years when I hated my father and thought him my mortal enemy, I had more or less gloried in my identification with him. But if I were to become somebody Joseph did not know, I would have to cut loose from that overwhelming persona and start being a recognizably different individual. It was one of the scariest things I have ever tried to do, for it seemed as if to be Not-Reinhold was to be Nobody, and I felt like a newborn infant left alone in intergalactic space.

But I concentrated on a single idea—namely, that being Not-Reinhold did not automatically mean that I became Nobody. There were other alternatives. Unknown, as yet, but subject to exploration (if I could nerve myself to do it). The most deeply rooted idea in my mind was that to be different from my father was to be defenseless, but this had not been *proved*. It might not be true. And the most obvious way to make a start would be to renounce that inherited habit of self-pity.

It was a struggle and it still is. When I am disappointed or frustrated, self-pity wells up inside me with the incredible swiftness of milk boiling over. But I found that if I could recognize it for what it was, and slap it down, I had a lot of extra energy at my disposal that used to be wasted in monotonous complaints. Thinking became possible, and the upshot of the thinking was that there was no use getting locked into a power struggle with Joseph, ineffably tempting though my combative nature found the prospect. I could contest his divorce suit with every chance of success—or so the Ironing Board said—but I could not force him to have another try at living together, which was the thing that would have been most reassuring to our daughter.

The circumstance of being powerless in the area where I least wished to be so led naturally into thinking about the whole question of power. "Power," said Henry Kissinger, "is the ultimate aphrodisiac." But an aphrodisiac is, like alcohol and drugs, an artificially enhancing agent you put into yourself from the outside. In my situation, there was only one person over whom I could hope to have any power, and that was myself.

A thing exists, the philosophers say, in terms of its opposite, and it is my belief that nobody really understands power who does not examine and upon occasion experience powerlessness. Upon occasion. Permanent powerlessness corrupts as much as absolute power. The real aficionados of power, of whom there are not many, understand that there is no satisfaction in it—it is just an ever-receding will-o'-the-wisp—unless it is won in a contest between equals.

The amateurs of power conceive of it as the mowing down of people who have no way of defending themselves, and the category of the amateurs includes anti-Semites, racists, totalitarian dictators, the C.I.A. and carpet bombers. But going after that kind of triumph is like trying to nourish oneself on sawdust. Appetite is not quieted by sawdust. Stalin had more power than almost anyone else in history, but he ended up with rocks in his head. And the most significant contest between equals sometimes takes place within the self—the contest between old habit and new insight.

Joseph was going to impose his will on me. He was, in

After seven weeks in the hospital, she was released and when the fall term opened at the Slade, she went back. She was so weak that in the beginning, she could only stay at school for twenty minutes a day, but the administration at the Slade provided a cot where she could lie down, and although she could barely walk, she would not let me accompany her to the school or send her in a taxi. She went alone on the bus.

After she got out of the hospital, we moved to a much better apartment, but the winter of 1969–70 was grim. She woke up every morning with vertigo, nausea and double vision, and it plunged her into despair. It shook me to the core to witness that despair, and I could find no words in my extensive Liberal Arts vocabulary that would mitigate it. Nevertheless, her capacity for recovery was awesome. She would always emerge—sooner rather than later—from the black pit, and then she would take my hand and say, "We'll manage"—and this became a kind of watchword for us.

She was in the hospital again in February of 1970, but this time it was less serious. And, in fact, that seemed to be the turning point. From then on—stubbornly, inch by determined inch—she forged ahead, and in 1971 she was graduated from the Slade, not without encomia. But although she came through her physical ordeal, there was an emotional ordeal that also had to be weathered. In August of 1970, I went to the United States to sign the divorce papers and learned by inadvertence of the affair that Joseph had been having almost since our arrival in the midwest. In September Celia received a brief note from her father saying that he had remarried.

And then the dam burst. It was the beginning, for my daughter, of a long period of intense emotional disturbance which took the form of a blazing hostility to me.

"You didn't do enough to stop it!" she cried. "You could have stopped it, but you didn't try!"

It was a sign of how deeply upset she was that she—normally a perfectly rational young person—could not take in the fact that I could not stop it because I did not know about it. All the time that she had been keeping the secret of her father's plan to remarry, she had apparently hoped desperately that the remarriage would, in the end, not take place. When it did, her anger and despair were directed, not at the person who had given her the secret to keep, but at the one from whom it had had to be kept. But family patterns tend to repeat themselves, unless consciously interrupted, and there was a rough justice in this seeming irrationality. The scorn and reproach my daughter heaped on me were a faithful echo of the scorn and reproach she had heard me heaping on Joseph for not having stood up to Becky. My chickens were coming home to roost.

This recognition, however, did not make it any the less a terrible time. I loved her so much, and we had been so close during the period when she was recovering from the second go-round with the tumor. Now to have become the target of her implacable hatred seemed more than flesh and blood could bear. Fortunately, I had made friends since my arrival in England and they provided both support and sound advice, as did the doctors who had pulled Celia through and gotten to be very fond of her.

"Be patient," they counseled. "Just wait. She will get over it."

In the meantime, however, there were agonizing scenes, and more than one midnight I walked the quiet streets of our neighborhood in tears because she had metaphorically torn me limb from limb for no greater provocation than my having mispronounced somebody's name. She for her part would lock herself in her room in a state of impotent fury because the torrents of rage she poured out on me failed completely to give her surcease from the torment in which she was living.

"Fortune favors the prepared mind."

My daughter's anger would wear off. It would exhaust itself by its own intensity. When it did, I had to be ready to work out a satisfactory relationship with her on the basis of her being well, not ill. The first part of the preparation was to try to accept the painful fact that I was not unique. Women who are abandoned by their husbands for somebody else after years of marriage are a dime a dozen. I was not a romantic heroine occupying stage front and center. I was an indistinguishable member of a sisterhood.

Like other members of the sisterhood, I had clapped the back of the hand to the forehead and staggered to the nearest sofa upon first learning that I had been supplanted; and from there on in, I was gnawed and chewed up by a corrosive envy of the departed husband and his new spouse, living so felicitously and cosily together while I struggled alone with problems about which I had been told for years not to bother my pretty head. Like other members of the sisterhood, too, I had been a prey to obsessive fantasies of getting my own back. One of the most idiotic of these fantasies was that I would marry an Englishman of title, so that—if Joseph and I ever met again, which we never have—he would have to call me Lady Margaret, and *that* would stick in his crop!

One primary mistake the sisterhood is very prone to make, and I made it. The mistake is to cry out to the child or children, "Be on my side! Admit that whatever I may have done that was bad, it was never so bad as what *he* has done!" When the ego has been razed to the ground like Carthage by a public rejection in favor of someone else, the temptation to rebuild it the cheap way—by getting endorsements from the outside—is well-nigh irresistible. But children know in their bones what their elders are often unwilling to face—namely, that for an adult, ego, like conscience, is strictly a problem for the owner.

Intellectually, I knew that I had no right to ask my daughter to be a partisan, particularly since she had been so dangerously ill. But the temptation of Saint Anthony was a mere bagatelle compared to the urges that swept over me to say, "Be on my side!" When I was in the grip of one of these urges, I prayed, like the saint, "Lord, make me chaste, but not yet." Hence, though my daughter's anger was sometimes sparked off by the merest trivia, such as her not liking something I had cooked for her, it was basically entirely justified. It was not for me to demand her loyalty. I would have to earn it. It was not already earned. But it took me a long time to assimilate this on the spontaneous, nonintellectual level—which is the one that counts. In the meantime, if she inflicted pain on me, I also inflicted pain on her.

Time, the great healer.

As both the doctors and the friends had predicted, my daughter's hostility did eventually exhaust itself; and then I had to let her tell me—and be willing to listen with all defenses down—what she really thought about me. This she imparted in several conversations we happened to have, and to say that it was startling and an eye-opener is a classic of understatement. I had always taken it for granted that I had been a good mother because I had consciously tried to be so; but my daughter's childhood, from her point of view, was a rather different proposition from what, in moments of self-congratulation, I had assumed.

When I was a child and a young person, I had boiled with helpless rage at Reinhold's puritan zest for denying and withholding. As when he forbade me to swim at the Knights

of Columbus pool. Or raised such hell about my having
dates. I had quite correctly assessed these denials as emotional self-indulgence on his part, and not the high and holy
discipline—imposed with no thought of anything but my
own good—which he tried to pretend they were. I learned
from my daughter, however, that I had done the same thing
to her that my father had done to me—the self-indulgent,
dishonestly represented "Thou shalt not." Perhaps not so
often as my father, for I was not bursting at the seams from
the tension of a wretched marriage. But often enough.

I had also taken it for granted, without giving it a second
thought, that simply by not being a recluse like Annie, I had
virtually guaranteed that my daughter would have a happy
childhood. People came and went in our house all the time,
and they were very nice people. Besides, there were the wit-
ticisms, the gaiety, the affectionate teasing.

"But there was always a breath of coldness," my daughter said.

I was as utterly silenced by the stark truth of this statement as I had been many years before when I had told Henry
Simon that I never thought of him as Jewish and he had
replied, "That's a very anti-Semitic remark." The coldness
my daughter felt came from my self-concern—the primacy I
automatically gave to my own problems. Perhaps the self-
absorption was to some extent, though not entirely, an un-
avoidable aspect of my being a writer; but children cannot see
their parents in context. All my daughter knew, in her forma-
tive years, was that she felt a chill. The outlines of the Girl in
the Glacier were still discernible.

It was when she talked about my drinking, however, that
I flinched the most.

"The worst part," she said, "was that you never had
hangovers. I'd be frightened to death by the kind of things
you said and the way your face looked when you got into one

of your rages, but the next morning you'd get up and eat breakfast and drive me to school, and I was supposed to pretend that nothing had happened.

"If," she added, "you'd been sick and shaking and full of remorse and guilt, it would have been easier."

Even when I thought the drinking was doing her no harm—when I was sitting and sipping for long hours in front of the fireplace and believed her to be tranquilly asleep upstairs—it caused her anxiety, for something in my manner told her that my addiction to alcohol was not a subject I would permit her to discuss.

It was harrowing to have to give up certain pleasant illusions I had had about myself as a parent. Chagrin is not a voluptuous sensation; but the wintry smile upon the face of Truth is, after all, a smile. Celia let me see that though she had always admired me, she had equally always found me formidable; but there was one compensation about this shearing-away of illusion and that was the discovery that my daughter is not vindictive. Once having said what she thought, she let the matter drop—something her mother had by no means had the capacity to do.

The year after she was graduated from the Slade, she went to Paris for eight months to study in an atelier, and while she was away we were able, because many of the bumpy spots in our relationship had been smoothed down, to have a marvelous correspondence. I have always had a fondness for the old-fashioned art of letter writing, and it was a joy to discover that this taste is something my daughter and I have in common. And while she was in Paris I went over several times to spend the weekend with her, and those weekends were occasions of such unflawed companionability that I shall remember them for the rest of my life.

The fairy-tale ending?

They lived happily ever after?

Probably not. The essence of life is problem-solving; and my daughter and I will certainly continue, separately or together, to have problems. That is the nature of things. But one problem, at least, has been surmounted. Good old Mother has been de-fanged.

Does it all add up to anything? Was there any point or meaning to those many years of being the kind of wife and mother who scorns cake mixes—while at the same time struggling, as a writer, to make a point about political morality that was being expressed a little before its time? I can only say that the two seemingly disparate aspects of my life actually reinforced each other, all along the way. The comforts of intimacy and domesticity assuaged some of the loneliness of writing. And when the crunch came of my daughter's illness and the breakup of my marriage, I was glad that, as a professional person, I was not a stranger to rejection, frustration and disappointment. I was not tempered steel, when the twin disasters came along, but at least I was a little bit stronger than a hairpin.

I have not emerged with any recipe for how to live in today's world. A few prosy little snippets I hug to my bosom, but I have never had the requisite strength of intellect—or a sufficient educational background—to weld them together into a structured philosophy. And perhaps no such strenuous effort is necessary. After World War II, the United States embarked on a huge but unacknowledged social experiment—the experiment being to jettison morality and the traditional code of ethics as no longer necessary in a society that was swimming in money. Today, some thirty years later, it is evident that never has the Judeo-Christian ethic been so completely validated as it has been by what has happened in our country since that ethic was informally but decisively junked.

Looking back now, it seems to me that Nixon's Checkers speech in 1952 was, like the Hiss case, one of those turning points in history which is not recognized as such at the time it happens. In truth, that speech was a Great Divide, for America was a different country after it took place from the country it had been before. Up until then, the cardinal rule in American politics had always been that you must not get found out. Skulduggery, yes; but if you got found out you were finished.

After the Checkers speech, however, it no longer mattered for a politician if he got found out. Should his sins come to light, he could go on television with a totally fake piece of oratory and receive not only instant absolution, but even a great deal of applause. The Checkers speech was thus a watershed. On one side of the watershed the bad apples, if they were discovered, were hoicked out of the barrel. On the other side—the side on which we have been living for the last quarter of a century—the bad apples, though discovered, were just left there.

American political life has never been a phenomenon which caused joy and ecstasy among the saints in heaven. Nevertheless it did always have a pendulumlike motion of corruption-reform-corruption-reform. But the effect of the anti-Communist hysteria after the war was to arrest the pendulum on the corruption side of the arc. The consent of the governed was secured by persuading a great many people that the Richard Nixons, Joe McCarthys and Congressional investigating committees were saving us from revolutionaries. But in terms of underlying social purpose—of which the opportunistic witch-hunters were sublimely unaware—the real target was not the revolutionaries in our midst, but the reformers. The United States, once it was established, had always been too rich and too fortunate to have given birth to a genuinely threatening revolutionary movement. Reformers, however, it had always had—the canaries in the coal mine whose agitated behavior signaled the approach of lethal gases. If morality and ethics were to be neutralized, the canaries had to be silenced.

Thus, when the Howdy-Doody babies reached maturity, they found an American society that seemed to be brimming with movement and action. There was a civil rights crusade (which ultimately petered out) and a war in Vietnam (which kept going year after year). Changes in taste and behavior succeeded each other with bewildering rapidity. But underneath all the apparent swirl of action, there was an unnatural calm. The pendulum was still. The canaries were dead. The rebellion of my daughter's college generation—at Berkeley and Columbia, and in other places—was perhaps an instinctive recoil from the stagnation, the death-in-life which underlay a seemingly fast-paced activity.

We older Americans allowed ourselves to be saddled with the institutionalized lie because we thought it was a necessary part of a technological civilization. (But is it? Or do we merely suffer from paralyzed imagination?) We thought we could "adjust" to the institutionalized lie. But the lie destroys communication, even when it is believed. Perhaps especially when it is believed. And when people are cut off from communication, they suffer all kinds of derangements, from insomnia to psychosis.

At the opposite pole from the institutionalized lie is the fabric of trust. When a society has an acknowledged and official code of ethics and when a sufficient number of people are loyal to it, a fabric of trust is created. A fabric of trust means that doors can be left unlocked, the streets are safe, goods laid out for sale will not be appropriated without payment, parks and public buildings will not be vandalized and

privacy will not be invaded by rooms being bugged unbe-
knownst to the occupants.

"What does it matter if I steal from a multinational?"

How many times one has heard this question asked! The
answer is that it does matter, for the issue is not whether the
multinational is hurt, but whether the fabric of trust is damaged. And it is. There is no individual in our society, however seemingly small and insignificant, whose actions do not
have an effect for either good or bad on the fabric of trust.
The multinationals bear a heavy responsibility for the maintenance of the institutionalized lie, but it does not strengthen
the fabric of trust to steal from them. The most practical way
to protect a fabric of trust is to hoick the political bad apples
out of the barrel as soon as they are discovered, for it is the
political bad apples who make possible the dictatorship of the
multinationals.

Upon those who have any kind of political idealism, a
materialistic society imposes two punishments. One is hostility. The other—less generally recognized—is condescension.
I have had the top of my head patted by hard-nosed journalists and what used to be called bomber liberals until it is
worn right down to the level of my eyebrows. But in that part
of my brain which has survived the kindly, dismissive hands
of the experts on *realpolitik*, I entertain a few generalized no-
tions—and one such is that there is a connectedness between
things.

Nothing happens in a vacuum. You start in with character assassination—justifying it on the grounds that there
might be Communists in government—and somewhere in
the course of history, the qualifying adjective disappears and
you end up with the real thing. Watergate began slouching
toward Bethlehem to be born when it became part of the po-

litical canon that Whittaker Chambers was a truthful man. "The line between the Hiss trial and the Watergate hearings is a direct one," says the English journalist Godfrey Hodgson in his recent book, *In Our Time*, subtitled *America from World War II to Nixon*.

In a consuming society, however, where very little happens that has not been engineered, everything possible is done to obscure the connectedness of things. Events which are in actuality related are presented to the public as completely dissociated. They are more startling and dramatic that way. Disconnectedness is often achieved by what is called "closing the book." The book is closed on Watergate. The book is closed on Vietnam. The book is closed on McCarthyism. And with the unchecked proliferation of terror weapons, the book is also closed on the future. Hence there is no place to live except in the present, and the headline events of the present—dissociated from either past or future—are felt as one shock after another. The general public is thus kept continually off balance, and a public which is off balance is much more easily manipulated than one which knows the score.

"Without vision, the people perish," and "vision" does not have to mean simply a bright view of the future. It can also mean an accurate perspective on the past. There is perhaps no connection it is more important to see than the connection between the McCarthy witch-hunt and the widespread breakdown of morality which has subsequently characterized American life. A great many people were unhappily conscious during the McCarthy period that the tactics used against the victims were unfair and unethical, but they compartmentalized the witch-hunt in their minds as "merely political." Compared to the whole population, the victims were few in number and there was the huge area of nonpolitical life to be got on with.

Life itself, however, flows and is sequential and punishes those who try to compartmentalize it. Thus if, for any reason whatsoever, moral standards are conspicuously and unprecedentedly breached in one area of society, such as the political, it will follow as the night the day that those standards will start collapsing all down the line—in sports, entertainment, education, the armed forces, business and government. Ironically enough, the domino theory which was supposed to justify the war in Vietnam was best exemplified here at home when the mindless destruction of reputations and livelihoods by Congressional investigators proved later on to have been an open sesame to the mindless destruction of life and property by muggers, vandals, rapists and mass murderers.

When my ex-husband talked about his job, he used sometimes to refer to what he called "preventive administration." This meant surveying past and present, deducing therefrom what of good or bad was likely to happen in the future, and taking steps to ensure that the bad was forestalled and the good brought to fruition. In the conduct of government, a good example of preventive administration would be to hold the C.I.A. morally responsible for its actions and sharply to delimit its supply of money, so as to spare the public, in future, those well-nigh incredible revelations which have done so much to keep people off balance.

Incidentally, it can readily be seen—when one thinks in terms of preventive administration—that it does the nation no good at all when good-natured but stupid men like Eisenhower and Ford succeed to the Presidency. Such men do not have the intellectual power to administer preventively. Eisenhower has been much praised for the speech he gave, on almost his last day in office, about the military-industrial complex; but it took him eight years—and he at the very heart and center of things—to discover that that baleful alliance existed.

It would be nice to conclude this book with a thundering of kettledrums and shrilling of trumpets, affirming American idealism in accents heard from here to Tierra del Fuego. But I have very little faith in my compatriots' idealism. I do have a modest faith, however, in their pragmatism. Nobody has ever written about the Americans who has not commented on their practicality. From de Toqueville on, it has been agreed by all observers that Americans do not care for abstract concepts (which is bad luck for me), but are interested only in making things work.

We have had a decades-long experiment in trying to maintain the outward form of a democracy without any inner core of ethical standards. It is now obvious that the experiment did not work. Q.E.D. But, as the old song title goes, "What Shall We Do After the Orgy?" On purely practical grounds, the fabric of trust recommends itself, for where it can be maintained, it saves time, energy and money.

To be sure—as a number of writers have already pointed out—the American streak of practicality and respect for know-how has led to our being victimized by the whole idea of expertise. In Lyndon Johnson's administration, only the President was supposed to be in command of "all the facts" about foreign policy and therefore only he was presumed to be capable of conducting that policy. With what results, the world knows. And snowed under by science and technology, we have genuflected humbly before the fellow who knows how to isolate a virus.

But what is the end in view? The end in view is not to be thrown off balance. Not to be easily manipulated. The end in view is to trust the soundness of one's own judgment and to hell with the opinion polls. For that, all you need to know is the score, and the score is there to be known. It has been there for a long time. "Whatsoever ye do even unto the least of these, ye do also unto Me." Though poetically expressed, it is a very practical sentiment, for it focuses attention on the connectedness of things and thus points in the direction of preventive administration.